ALL THE LOVERS IN THE NIGHT

Mieko Kawakami is the author of the internationally bestselling novel *Breasts and Eggs*, a *New York Times* Notable Book of the Year and one of *TIME*'s Best 10 Books of 2020, and the highly acclaimed *Heaven*, her second novel to be translated and published in English, which Oprah Daily described as written 'with jagged, visceral beauty'. Born in Osaka, Kawakami made her literary debut as a poet in 2006, and in 2007 published her first novella, *My Ego, My Teeth, and the World*. Known for their poetic qualities, their insights into the female body, and their preoccupation with ethics and modern society, her books have been translated into over twenty languages. Kawakami's literary awards include the Akutagawa Prize, the Tanizaki Prize, and the Murasaki Shikibu Prize. She lives in Tokyo.

Also by Mieko Kawakami

Breasts and Eggs

Heaven

Mieko Kawakami

ALL THE LOVERS IN THE NIGHT

*Translated from the Japanese
by Sam Bett and David Boyd*

PICADOR

First published 2022 by Europa Editions, New York

First published in paperback 2022 by Picador

This paperback edition published 2023 by Picador
an imprint of Pan Macmillan
The Smithson, 6 Briset Street, London EC1M 5NR
EU representative: Macmillan Publishers Ireland Ltd, 1st Floor,
The Liffey Trust Centre, 117–126 Sheriff Street Upper,
Dublin 1, D01 YC43
Associated companies throughout the world
www.panmacmillan.com

ISBN 978-1-5098-9829-9

Copyright © Mieko Kawakami 2011
Translation copyright © Mieko Kawakami 2022
Translation by Sam Bett and David Boyd 2022

The right of Mieko Kawakami to be identified as the
author of this work has been asserted by her in accordance
with the Copyright, Designs and Patents Act 1988.

Originally published in Japan as *Subete mayonaka no koibito tachi*

All rights reserved. No part of this publication may be reproduced,
stored in a retrieval system, or transmitted, in any form, or by any means
(electronic, mechanical, photocopying, recording or otherwise)
without the prior written permission of the publisher.

Pan Macmillan does not have any control over, or any responsibility for,
any author or third-party websites referred to in or on this book.

1 3 5 7 9 8 6 4 2

A CIP catalogue record for this book is available from the British Library.

Printed and bound by CPI Group (UK) Ltd, Croydon, CR0 4YY

This book is sold subject to the condition that it shall not, by way of
trade or otherwise, be lent, hired out, or otherwise circulated without
the publisher's prior consent in any form of binding or cover other than
that in which it is published and without a similar condition including
this condition being imposed on the subsequent purchaser.

Visit **www.picador.com** to read more about all our books
and to buy them. You will also find features, author interviews and
news of any author events, and you can sign up for e-newsletters
so that you're always first to hear about our new releases.

ALL THE LOVERS IN THE NIGHT

Why does the night have to be so beautiful?

As I walk through the night, I remember what Mitsutsuka said to me. "Because at night, only half the world remains." I count the lights. All the lights of the night. The red light at the intersection, trembling as if wet, even though it isn't raining. Streetlight after streetlight. Taillights trailing off into the distance. The soft glow from the windows. Phones in the hands of people just arriving home, and people just about to go somewhere. Why is the night so beautiful? Why does it shine the way it does? Why is the night made up entirely of light?

The music flows from the earphones filling my ears, filling me—it becomes everything. A lullaby. A gorgeous piano lullaby. What a wonderful piece of music. It really is. It's my favorite piece by Chopin. Did you like it too, Fuyuko? Yeah. It's like the night is breathing. Like the sound of melted light.

The light at night is special because the overwhelming light of day has left us, and the remaining half draws on everything it has to keep the world around us bright.

You're right, Mitsutsuka. It isn't anything, but it's so beautiful that I could cry.

1

D id you get the boxes?"

When Hijiri Ishikawa called, I'd just finished my work for the morning and was filling a pot with water to make a little spaghetti for lunch.

"Yeah, last night. But I haven't opened them yet."

Once I had the pot on the burner, I switched the phone from between my chin and shoulder into my left hand, went back into the other room and crouched down in front of the two cardboard boxes that had come the night before, then gave one of them a little push. It didn't budge.

"No rush. There's a lot in there. You've got tons of time before the deadline, but it's still a lot."

"Don't worry," I said. "I'm used to it now."

"You think?" Hijiri teased. "Sometimes you can be okay with something, then the next day comes and it's a totally different story."

"Yeah, I know, but I feel like I've got this under control," I laughed. "Maybe because I haven't opened anything yet."

"Why do they always have to use so many sources? Can't these people write anything on their own? I guess they're all like that, but this one's practically all quotes, right? The author probably wrote less than half the book."

On the other end of the line, I heard Hijiri laughing through her nose. "I had a hard time just getting everything to the front desk. I was honestly worried that they might not give me workers' comp if I threw my back out."

"But we got lucky," I said. "I can't believe that all the books we needed were available from the same place. It's like a dream."

Hijiri laughed.

"You're right about that," she said. "By the way, I took the liberty of looking over the first proofs."

I poured a warmed-up packet of meat sauce over the spaghetti and ate my lunch. When I was done, I pulled my bangs back with a headband, took my pencil in my right hand, and set up my makeshift bookrest (a large drawing board that I bought at an art store in Shinjuku and kept propped up at an angle on my long-neglected Greek dictionary and vocabulary book, and told myself would be a temporary solution until I got a proper bookrest, though four years had gone by in the meantime), sliding it up against my stomach as always to make sure it stayed put, then stared at the pages before me, working my way through the manuscript, questioning one element of text after another.

When I got tired, I'd do some stretches, alternating between rotating my neck and arms, then go into the kitchen and make myself a hot cup of tea, letting it cool as I sipped it slowly.

I felt as if I could sit there and work at my desk as long as necessary, but I knew that unless I took regular breaks here and there I'd start to overlook things when I least expected it, so I made sure to take a break every two hours. Once I'd relaxed for a good moment, I went back to my desk and repeated the same process, again and again.

As I worked my way through, I used the reference table that I kept to the left of the manuscript, which summarized the interpersonal relationships, timeline, and plot at a glance, checking for inconsistency with what the characters in the novel were actually saying in the relentless stream of dialogue. This novel in particular, which I had started reading two days earlier, had introduced so many people over a number of years, too many names to count. Since the story took place in a large mansion, I also had a sheet with the floorplan on it.

The name of the corset. Whether or not plumerias have white flowers. Is Charles Dickens *really* Charles Dickens?

Using my dictionaries and the internet to double-check proper nouns and historical facts, I would go over the text multiple times, just to make sure, whenever something tripped me up, even a little. Along the way, I found various kinds of spelling errors, making corrections with my pencil and flagging each one with a question mark.

There were always lines that defied comprehension. When I found myself stumped as to whether something like this was intentional, or maybe some quirk of the author's, I emailed Hijiri and asked her for advice. When we couldn't solve it between the two of us, I left a note for the author in tiny script, asking for clarification.

Three years ago, at the end of April, I quit the company that I had started working for just after graduating college.

It was a little publisher that nobody had ever heard of, where they produced books that made you wonder who would ever read them. The only thing that they had going for them was their name.

The specifics of any job in publishing will vary slightly, depending on the scope and personality of the company, but on a basic level, it's all about making and selling books. One of the various jobs required to make that happen involves reading and re-reading the many sentences that ultimately make up a book, searching for any typos and linguistic or factual errors—in other words, proofreading. That was what I did for this small company. I was a proofreader, spending every moment of my day, from morning to night, hunting for mistakes.

Although I'd quit only after thinking things over from all possible angles, I'm still not sure why I felt like I had to leave. I feel sort of stupid saying I was tired of dealing with people, but when it comes down to it, I guess there's no other way to put it.

From a young age, I couldn't bring myself to contribute to conversations like a normal person, much less socialize or go out with people, and I was never able to acclimate to the particular atmosphere of that little office. At first, my coworkers invited me out for dinner or drinks, but I always declined, offering a string of vague excuses, and at some point they stopped asking. Before I knew it, I'd been left entirely alone. No one ever spoke to me unless they needed something, and when candy or cookies showed up during the workday, the box always went right past me and moved along to the next desk. It would have been one thing if the others had literally left me alone, but their indifference, over time, showed hints of bitterness, which became apparent in their silence and their looks, to the point where going to work became difficult to bear.

Once I was spending all of my time alone, not talking to anyone, I started to hear people whispering about me at odd moments in the day. A few of my coworkers even used a secret language that they thought I didn't understand to talk about me right in front of me, making jokes at my expense. Once this had become normal, they started asking me all kinds of nosy questions that had nothing to do with work. Aren't you going to get married? Why not? What do you do on your days off? I said that I stayed home. They laughed, practically snorting. What'll you do with all the money that you're saving? This kept going, one question on top of another. If I was silent, unsure of what I was supposed to say, the girls seated nearby would prick their ears up, careful not to look away from their computer screens and trying to keep their lips sealed as they laughed without making a sound.

Most of the questions came from a woman in her fifties, as if she were the leader of the group. She was the sort of person whose manner of speaking conveyed an immense pride in having built a family along with her career, raising two wonderful children. I had been seated next to her since my first day at the company (and if I hadn't quit, I'm sure this never would have changed until the day that she retired). None too shy about speaking her mind, she waited for those moments when it was just the two of us. Apparently offended by what she saw in me as the self-absorption of a single woman who did nothing with her life but work, she reminded me at length, sighing periodically, of how much effort it required her to keep her life afloat, and how easy things were for people like me. When the other girls were around, she never said anything of the sort, but picked on me instead, to win their favor.

The more I worked in silence, and the longer I stayed at the company, the worse it felt to be there. One day, I overheard two of the new girls, who were almost ten years younger than I was, saying I was only playing nice because I had nowhere else to go, that I must be allergic to fun—as if I was to blame for never turning down a job or ever being late for a deadline. This made me so confused. What kind of fun was I supposed to be having? If somebody asked me to do a job, and I didn't want to do it, what was the right way to turn them down? If I thought about things long enough, I would always lose track of my own feelings, which left me with no choice but to proceed as usual, without taking any action. Maybe the girls were right about me having no place else to go, about there being nothing fun about my life.

That was when I got a call from Kyoko.

"The person they've been using ended up quitting, and they're looking for someone who can step in right away."

I hadn't seen Kyoko in years, and this was definitely the first time she'd ever called me, so at first I had no idea what was going on. However, since she insisted that there was something urgent that she wanted to discuss, I agreed to meet up with her to talk that weekend.

Kyoko was an editor who had worked for ages at the company, but she quit a few years after I started in order to go into business for herself. She described her work as editorial production.

"I started picking up a lot of work on the side, and now I have a team of people working for me. We do photography, editing, design work, writing projects. I don't even know what kind of business I'm running anymore."

She opened her mouth wide and laughed. It was a sort of conspicuous laugh that I remembered well. Then there was the funny way she said my last name—Irie—that made me feel a bit nostalgic.

Kyoko had gained so much weight that I failed to recognize her when she walked into the cafe, but the supple skin of her perfectly made-up face gave me the feeling that she looked much younger than the last time we had met. When I started at the company, I was twenty-two, and I'm pretty sure that she was thirty-two, which would make her just over forty. Not that she didn't have her fair share of wrinkles, normal for her age, but all the same, she had a certain liveliness about her.

Rolling up the sleeves of the thin black sweater she wore over a soft-looking white blouse, Kyoko looked right at me and said that it was turning out to be a hot one. Unable to respond while looking her in the eye, I let my gaze fall to where her chin met the skin of her neck, nodding at intervals as I listened to what she had to say.

"I don't know what things are like over there now, but do you have any room for some work on the side?"

A major publisher that Kyoko had been working with was looking for someone who could proofread on a freelance basis, which made her think of me, she said. As it so happened, we had only had lunch together once, with a few other people from the company, but had never shared anything close to a conversation, just the two of us. We may have worked in the same office, but I barely ever spoke with anybody there, just quietly went about doing my job, and certainly had no connection with her. So I was less happy than mystified, maybe even a little uneasy, to hear that her thoughts had turned to me after all these years.

"I could run it through my company, but I'm a little hesitant to make my team any bigger. Anyway, they're looking for somebody who has experience."

As she spoke, Kyoko played with a thick silver ring on her index finger. Her skin bulged above the ring's circumference. Looking at her hand, I took a sip of my black tea, then closed my lips and nodded a few times. The tea was lukewarm, with a bitter, powdery taste.

"I know you've got plenty on your plate at the office, and I don't mean to push, but this is a big company. You wouldn't have to worry about the work being sporadic. Plus, they're really flexible. Think of it as a part-time job. If you could carve out just a little time . . ."

I replayed the last words Kyoko said inside my head. *Carve out just a little time.* After I had started at the company and grown accustomed to my work, I stopped watching TV, unable to endure the frustration of not being able to correct the errors I found in the text appearing on the bottom of the screen. I didn't usually read books or listen to music. I had no friends to go out to eat with or to chat with for hours over the phone. Other than in extreme circumstances, I never brought work home, and was able to take care of all of my responsibilities, research included, during working hours. At the latest, I was always home by eight, in time to fix myself a simple dinner, after which I had nothing else to do.

How did I pass the stretch of several hours that came night after night before I went to sleep? And how did I fill the vast expanse of time before starting my workday?

My memory was blank. All I could remember were the countless characters of text, printed in straight lines on white paper.

"That sounds nice to me," I said, after a pause.

When Kyoko heard me, she opened her eyes wide. Every inch of her face was smiling.

"That's great!"

I nodded and looked down at the floral pattern on my empty teacup.

"I'm so glad it'll work out," she said. "If anything comes up, don't hesitate to let me know, no matter when or what it is."

Grabbing a notebook from her bright orange leather bag, she asked me for my address and my email, which she wrote down swiftly with a thin silver pen.

"You should hear from them pretty soon. Thanks so much! It's a big help. I owe you one. I'll be in touch soon, okay?"

Kyoko drank the rest of her coffee and suggested we get going, so we got up and left the cafe. I tried paying for my share, but Kyoko said stop and smiled in a way that made her look a little worried. I apologized and bowed, returning my wallet to the tote bag slung over my shoulder. Ahead of me by then, she turned to say that she was glad that I was doing well and matched my pace for a few steps, then hailed a cab. Before she closed the door, she wished me luck and told me to give her a call if anything came up.

Hijiri Ishikawa worked at the publisher that Kyoko had introduced me to, in the proofreading department at their giant office.

She did her share of proofreading as well, but she mostly

acted as liaison for the freelance proofreaders and the people involved in external production, responsible for sending galleys, manuscripts and files.

As far as the job was concerned, we could have taken care of everything via email, courier, and the occasional phone call, but a few months after we made it through our first winter together, Hijiri started calling me up all the time, whenever she had something to ask, or even when she didn't, just to see how things were coming along.

I met Hijiri soon after starting the side job that Kyoko had arranged for me. We were at a party just after New Year's that the company had put together to give the in-house proofreaders and the freelancers a chance to mingle, introduce themselves and get to know each other better. After gazing at the invitation that Kyoko had forwarded to me, I spent at least three days debating whether I should go before deciding to make an appearance.

Hijiri's hair, cut short enough that you could see her ears, was dyed a pretty shade of brown. Her makeup was absolutely perfect. I'd never seen such a meticulously made-up face that closely before, and not in a magazine or on a poster or on TV, but in person. A unique aura surrounded her, something like a special layer of light that gave her a brightness greater than the space around her.

I got the sense that Hijiri was always straight with people, no matter whom she was talking to. Around the end of the event, she got into an argument with the male editor sitting next to her, over some tiny little thing, but in the end she shut him up entirely. From two seats away, I witnessed the entirety of the exchange. I remember feeling an excitement I was unable to understand, something about the way she unleashed provocative expressions so effectively, the confidence of her delivery and the way she made her point, how she maintained composure, in those moments where the man raised his voice defensively, as she looked around and smiled. Quick off the mark, she was able to suss out the mood of any situation, adding a smart joke here and there to make people laugh. It only took me a couple of hours to realize that she was a woman of talents beyond anything I could imagine—even though I was a stranger to such talents myself.

Hijiri and I were the same age, and we were both from Nagano, though from different parts of the prefecture. Aside from these two points and our gender, I couldn't find anything else we had in common, but for some reason she was very kind to me.

Not long after that January party, Hijiri and I began communicating regularly about the details of the work at hand. Sometimes I had to meet with her in person, to turn in a manuscript or confirm some detail, which always made me really nervous, but Hijiri didn't take my anxious feelings seriously, which actually helped me loosen up a bit. Little by little, I warmed up to talking about things unrelated to work. Most of the time, I was simply listening to Hijiri talk, but she insisted that I was fun to be around and laughed to show me that she really meant it, too. When I asked what part of me she thought was fun, she would simply say, "Part? Everything about you," then laugh again with delight, not giving me a real answer. I was never sure how to respond to this, so I'd say nothing and look down. But then Hijiri would tell me, "Don't worry. When I say you're fun, I'm talking about how I feel. I'm just saying that I enjoy your company. There's nothing to get upset about, even if it doesn't make sense to you," and give me a warm smile. I never talked that much compared to Hijiri, but now and then I'd lose track of the time and realize I was having fun as well, quietly surprised that I was capable of such a thing.

About a year after we had started meeting up for work,

after one of our in-person sessions, Hijiri asked me how things were going at my day job.

I did my best to tell her, in a roundabout way, how I found the work itself worthwhile, how I knew it was the right kind of work for me, but that the company wasn't the best environment. When I was finished with my roundabout response, Hijiri looked me in the eye and just said, "Is that right?" For a little while, we were both quiet. Her expression made it look like she was thinking about something. The fact that she wasn't saying anything made me worry that she thought I was complaining. Her question had been purely about work—as in the manuscripts I was working on right now, or what was in the offing, but I'd started venting about the company environment, which had nothing to do with her question and was certainly none of her concern. I panicked, fearful that I had disappointed her, or had even offended her. But I had no idea how to convey this hadn't been my intention. I lacked the confidence to speak well. I was certain that I had said too much already; I kept silent, unsure what I should do, but then Hijiri spoke up and said that maybe I should consider going freelance entirely.

"I know it's freelance, but it's not bad . . . I don't know the details of your current situation, in terms of pay, or health insurance, but I'm sure that someone who works as hard as you could handle four books a month and make yourself 300,000 yen. There'd be highs and lows, of course, but I think you could expect somewhere around there every month." Hijiri looked me in the eye. "It all depends how hard you work, I suppose."

When I realized that I hadn't actually hurt Hijiri's feelings, I was so relieved I could have sighed out loud, but there was more going on. Freelance, 300,000 a month, highs and lows, not to mention her evaluation of me as a hard worker. Some of the words that came out of her mouth left me confused, unable to speak.

"Well, what do you think?" she asked.

While she tried to get a read on me, I nodded several times and replayed what she had said inside my head. Going freelance as a proofreader . . . Hijiri had told me to consider it. This would mean quitting the company and spending all of my time on the work that I was currently doing on the side. I wouldn't have to go to an office anymore, but I could continue with my current work, at my own pace, in my own way—that was what Hijiri was proposing.

From now on, I could work from home, making my living as a freelance proofreader. I tried saying this several times inside my head. Up until that point, I don't think I'd ever once considered quitting the company, much less doing this work independently, but now that it had been put into words, words that I then whispered again in my own head, the possibility had somehow taken on a terribly realistic weight and reso-nance, to the point where I began to feel as if this were my only choice, that it had always been my only choice, a happy turn of events that made me feel like I could blush.

I thought about the office. The way things felt there. I asked myself what was so special about the place, aside from it being somewhere I could go to every day. Thin cardboard boxes of sweets, visibly displayed on the shelving unit to my left. Someone else's mug. A whiteboard that had basically turned gray. Computer screens. The sharp pain building in my tem-ples. The quiet hours exchanging words with no one, like a dark dream that never seemed to end. The shapes of the eyes of my coworkers. The clacking of the keyboards. In the midst of all these images, a brilliant white manuscript appeared, packed with freshly printed text just waiting to be read by me, and giv-ing off a certain warmth, but when I blinked its incandescent texture slipped into the reaches of a silence that I knew too well.

My annual salary was 3,200,000.

As nice as it was to collect a salary for finishing whatever work was given to me, it was like Hijiri had said. I was finally coming around to the idea that it was not entirely impossible for me to make a living as a freelancer—provided, that is, I was regularly given work. It had been about a year since I had started working on the side, and the number of manuscripts sent my way, as well as payment for my services, was fairly steady, but working in the privacy of my own home, just me and the manuscripts, slowly going over every word and every sentence, filled me with a satisfaction that was altogether different from doing the same work at the office.

"That would be incredible, if it worked out," I said, like I was talking to myself. I laughed a little. I didn't mean to, but unsure what kind of face I should be making, I started laughing, in an odd way that betrayed the fact that I was used to living my life in a daze, without giving anything much thought. Dark waves rolled through my chest, and I wiped my fingertips over and over with the oshibori on the table.

"We actually work with lots of freelance proofreaders," Hijiri said cheerfully. "Some of them have been at it more than twenty years."

"Twenty years?" I said.

"Yeah, twenty."

". . . But there'd be no, um, guarantee . . . I would have work to do every month . . . ?"

I worried about what Hijiri thought of me for asking this, but I had to ask. Dismissing my concerns, she made a serious face and fixed her gaze on me.

"That's a really, really important question," she said, nodding forcefully. "Think of it this way: like every other publisher, there's no month when we're not making books. I can't promise everything will go as planned, but the editorial director thinks very highly of your work, and he's always saying it'd be great if you could take on more. Seriously. So if you were to go freelance, and you could handle more galleys, it would be a massive help to us. That's the honest truth."

"Really?" I looked at Hijiri, a little perplexed.

"Really," she said a bit louder than necessary, as if to drive away my fears.

"Really?" I asked again, then let out a sigh. My entire face relaxed, and this time I was able to laugh normally.

"I love having people I can trust doing the work," Hijiri said, after a pause.

"Trust?"

"Yeah, trust," Hijiri said with a smile. "It's not the same as relying on someone. It's really different, actually. I mean, I guess it's all about both parties counting on each other."

I nodded.

"It's like they say, trust is a two-way street. Reliance can be one-sided, though. Know what I mean? One side depends on the other. That's not a partnership. And that's why relationships based on reliance are pretty unstable. One little hiccup and everything could disappear."

"Yeah."

"So what good is reliance when everything could fall apart because of some little bump or a change in the wind? That's not how trust works, though, at least not for me. With trust, I'm always giving something back for what I get. There's a balance."

As she spoke, Hijiri scratched the back of her ear.

"And once I trust somebody, that trust never fades."

I nodded quietly, listening to Hijiri.

"That's how it is. And for me, trust doesn't come from liking someone, or loving them. It has to come from how that person approaches their work."

"How they approach their work?" I asked.

"Exactly. That's the key. You can learn so much about a person from how they approach their work. Well, that's how I see it."

"You mean, how serious they are . . . that sort of thing?" I asked.

"Maybe," Hijiri said. For a few moments she stared up at the ceiling, like she was thinking, then nodded several times. "Maybe that's the simplest way to put it. And the type of work doesn't even matter. It could be housework, or working the register at a supermarket, or day trading, or physical labor, anything at all. And just like the content of the work doesn't matter, neither do the results. The thing about results—whether or not something turns out well—is that it's mostly about luck. Things like that can change. You can make people believe whatever you want. You can fool them like it's nothing. But you can't fool yourself, not really. That's why what matters is how you think about your work in your own lifetime, how much you respect it, how hard you're trying. Or tried. The people I trust are the ones who give work their all—I know it's a stupidly old-fashioned way to put it, but that's how I see it."

"So . . ." I said, then nodded a few times. ". . . How do you figure that out?"

"If I spend a little time with someone, talk, and look over their work, I can tell right away," Hijiri said with a grin.

"Just like that?"

"Just like that." She raised the corners of her lips, a look that underscored how obvious this was to her. "And those are the people for me—the only ones that I like." She was still grinning. "I guess I trust that feeling, whatever makes me like them. Though I don't know if it's really about like or love—I've never given much thought to love . . . But what ultimately lasts is something that can't simply change or disappear at any moment . . . It's trust."

Having said this, Hijiri looked deep into my eyes.

"Anyway, I trust you."

"Me?" I asked, surprised.

"Yes, you."

Seeing me surprised, Hijiri opened her eyes wide, laughed, and asked what I was so surprised about. I didn't know where to look, so I looked down, unable to look her in the face for some time.

"I trust the way you approach your work," she said. "And that means that I trust you . . . Sorry if that's a little confusing. But for me, no standard matters more." Hijiri smiled and shrugged. I looked at her and told her thank you in a quiet voice.

". . . You know how in our line of work," she said, "no matter what you do, no matter how hard you look, some mistakes always make it through? I mean, even if multiple people go over the same galley multiple times, for days on end, to the point where they can't read it anymore, no matter how much work everyone puts into it, no book is ever free of errors, right?"

"Right," I said. And that was the truth.

"You'll always, always find some kind of a mistake."

"Yeah."

"And if that's true, that means that there has never been a perfect book, and that no job can ever actually be finished. When a book comes out, a year can pass without any mistakes coming to light, but years later, you open it up and there it is: a misprint staring right back at you. It happens all the time, but every time, it's the worst feeling in the world, right? It's devastating, you've been completely and utterly abandoned."

"Absolutely."

"Like, do you know how hard I worked on that thing? It's literally the worst feeling in the world."

Hijiri said this like she really meant it.

"Yeah," I said. "Absolutely." And I really meant it too.

"Even though all of our experience tells us that there's no such thing as a book with zero mistakes, we still aim for that perfect book, don't we? A perfect book with no errors at all.

And maybe it's a battle that we're bound to lose before we even start, but it's not like we have any other choice, right?"

I nodded.

"I know we can't make something out of nothing," Hijiri said, "but the work we're doing is still really important. I don't claim to know anything about literature, or fiction, or criticism, but I'm proud of what I do . . . I don't know how to explain it, but there's something to the work we do. Something that really matters. And I get the sense you feel the same."

Hijiri sat there motionless, lips taut, like she was thinking about something.

"That's what I live for," Hijiri said. "It's everything."

For a minute, we sat there drinking our drinks. When a group of older ladies seated nearby burst out laughing, we both jumped in our seats, then caught each other smiling.

"I'll find a way to bring it up with the managing editor. For now, I'll just say you're exploring the idea of going freelance. I'll see if I can get a read on the situation. But I'm serious, okay? It'd mean a lot to us, if you were able to focus on our books like that. I know I've said it before, but we really talk about it all the time."

Hijiri looked at her wristwatch and said that she had to get going. The phone, handkerchief, and notepad that she had unpacked on the table now went back into her bag. Taking the receipt between her fingertips, she told me she would contact me when we were closer to the deadline, then waved her free hand and went outside.

So I decided to quit the company and become a freelance proofreader. My bosses told me that it was the worst possible time for me to leave. I almost backed down a few times, but there were no contractual impediments, and I was at a decent stopping point with the work that I was doing. Although I didn't give them a clear reason for leaving, over the course of several conversations, I finally managed to make it clear that I was done.

After I cleaned out my desk, filled out the necessary paperwork, said goodbye to the people I needed to say goodbye to, walked downstairs, and left the building, the strength drained from my shoulders, and the world practically tipped sideways. Setting my two paper bags onto the ground, I took a moment to stretch my back and exhaled deeply, then inhaled so deeply that my chest hurt. Once I repeated this a few times, a freshness I was sure I'd never known before spread slowly through my lungs, and I was filled with an awareness of the soft places inside me, spreading outward by degrees. It felt as if the flow of cars, no different than ever, and the greenness of the streetside vegetation, and the air itself were all a little more lucid than usual.

But I was only able to walk within that vivid scenery for a little while. As the company where I'd spent no small amount of time slipped into the distance the feeling that I had done something I could never undo clung to my back and began to pull me down. With every step I took, a veil of darkness came down over all I saw.

Shouldn't I have tried harder to make it work? Had I lost touch with reality, riding high on encouragement from Hijiri? I know I could have done more, tried harder, made it work. Everybody in this life has something they have to put up with. An uneasiness laced with regret climbed its way up my throat, nothing that a voice or sigh could shake.

2

Nine winters ago—on the night of my twenty-fifth birthday, at a little after eleven, I decided to go out for a walk.

I'm not sure what gave me the idea, but as I sat there, watching yet another uneventful birthday coming to an end, I had the sudden desire to go out and walk around. Sure, it would probably have been nice to bring a cake home (my birthday is Christmas Eve, so the city was full of cakes), or have a conversation with somebody, but going for a walk was the only thing that came to mind that I could do on my own.

That winter was so cold that my breath would turn white even indoors if I didn't keep the heat on. Shivering as I shed layers of pajamas, I put on a sweater and a pair of jeans over my underwear, pulled on a thick jacket, filled the space around my neck with a scarf, then headed out.

A tension ruled over the December air. Not a trace of wind swept over the earth, but looking up I saw the clouds were blowing by at a ferocious pace. For a little while, I just stood there, gazing up at the night sky. The layers and layers of clouds, not exactly white or gray, hung in the night sky like the outline of some kind of creature, enormous and moving without a sound, a sight that made my heart race. The brilliant white moon showed its face. It was a quiet birthday night. Hands in my jacket pockets, I started walking down the street, not another person in sight, but for some reason, it lifted my mood.

That night, everything was thrown into oddly sharp relief,

as if the pieces of the world before my eyes were telling me some kind of story. It was an entirely familiar scene, except the usual rows of houses, telephone poles and everything else seemed to shine with a triumphant light.

A planter by a front door, nothing inside but a mat of dead weeds devoid of color. Empty bottles and cans and plastic bags left in the basket of a rusty bicycle. These things contained a secret meaning that only I could understand.

As I carefully observed them one by one, each new thing that caught my eye created a soft sound inside of me. I felt as if the glow of night was sending me a message, secretly wishing me a happy birthday.

Every birthday since, I've gone out for a walk at night.

I eyed the calendar on my desk, remembering that first night I went out and walked around, but it was only April, over half a year until my next walk through the night.

I flipped through the calendar to December and looked at the picture of a snowy Christmas tree, then went back to April before flipping back to December again. It goes without saying, but that was as far as the calendar went. Apart from a few deadlines marked lightly in pencil, I had no plans whatsoever. It crossed my mind that I would probably never notice if the previous six months and the six months to follow had been switched around.

I made some food, ate it, washed the dishes, then returned to my work. Without taking a break, I reached the number of pages I had said that I would not exceed on a given day, so I turned off my desk light and did some stretches. Afterwards, I picked through the heap of laundry I had abandoned earlier, and was folding underwear and towels when my cell phone rang. Since nobody but Hijiri ever called me, I didn't need to check the display to know who it was, but it was rare for her to call so late. It was ten-thirty at night.

"What are you up to?" Hijiri asked, sounding like she was in a good mood today.

"Folding laundry," I said. Wherever Hijiri was calling from, it was pretty loud.

"Then what? Time for bed? Or are you going back to work?"

"I finished work a little while ago."

"Then how about coming out for a little bit?" Hijiri asked. "I just said goodbye to some people from work I was drinking with."

Hijiri told me the name of the place where she was. After hesitating for a moment, I wrote it down. I never went anywhere this late, except on my birthday, and I would have certainly refused if she had been with anybody else, but she was alone, so I had a hard time saying no.

"Don't worry if it's too much trouble," she said. "Actually, no. You should come out, even if it is too much trouble. You gotta get out sometimes. Not that I've ever asked you to come out at night before." Hijiri laughed. "We won't talk about anything serious. Come on, it'll be fun."

"Okay," I finally said. Once I'd double-checked with her what I had written down, we hung up. Then I let out a massive sigh, looked around the room for no real reason, and changed into jeans and a lightweight sweatshirt. I thought that I should probably wear something over this, but I had nothing that would qualify as a spring coat. As I hunted for another sweatshirt, this thought went through my mind. Every year, I told myself I needed a spring coat, but after getting this far without buying one, I figured that I probably never would. Spring coat . . . a coat for spring. For a moment there, I felt the urge to look up the precise definition—typical proofreader—but I put on my shoes and walked out the door.

The bar where Hijiri had asked me to meet her was the picture of chic, with lighting somewhere between amber and gold.

There weren't many other people around, which made it feel like it was even bigger. Soft music was playing from speakers in the ceiling.

When I showed up, Hijiri was already there, sitting at the far end of the counter. When she spotted me, she waved me over.

"You made it!" Hijiri laughed like she was thrilled and pulled out a chair for me.

She was wearing a red dress and a fluffy gray cardigan. The chest was embroidered with a spread of tiny beads that caught the light whenever she moved.

"Have you had a lot to drink?" I noticed that the glass in Hijiri's hand was already empty.

"You know how it is," Hijiri said, as if talking about somebody else. "I guess I always drink a lot, but today I'm really going for it. What do you want to drink?"

"Something without alcohol."

Ordering another of the same for herself, Hijiri got me a non-alcoholic mango cocktail.

"Do you, um, go out drinking with people from work a lot? Is that a regular thing?" I was feeling too nervous to look at her while I spoke, so I sort of looked around the room. "This place is really nice, huh?"

"This is maybe my second time here. And, no, we don't go out to drink that often. Just when somebody new joins the team, or when somebody leaves. And maybe the end of the year. I mean, sometimes a couple of us go out for a drink or two. Not like I need to tell you this, but proofreading is a lonely business, full of lonely people."

Hijiri gave me a big smile, looking genuinely happy. It felt softer than her usual smile.

"But the people above us, upstairs, in editing, where they make the books . . . I bet it's different for them. I know people in all the departments, and from what I hear, they're really something else up there. They spend a lot of time meeting up with all the great authors, just eating and drinking. Some of them can spend literally whatever they want."

"Really?"

"Well, I don't know for sure, but that's what I've heard."

"So the great authors are the ones who sell a lot of books?"

"I wonder," Hijiri said. "I don't work with them directly. I'm not sure. I guess so? Except, well, there are plenty of authors who don't sell at all but are supposedly great. You know how the prizes work, right?"

"Yeah."

"Some writers are great, but not successful. Then you get other writers who are successful, but not so great. I'm sure there's some sort of special principle behind it. Then again, I guess there are things like that everywhere. We get this all the time as women, right? Like, if you make plenty of money but don't have any kids, you might get called successful. But unless you have kids, no one will ever call you a great woman. You know what I mean?"

I nodded as I wiped my hands carefully with the oshibori.

"Well, in one way, the question of greatness definitely matters, if we're thinking about where our salaries are coming from, but as far as our work is concerned, it makes no difference. Because all manuscripts are equally fair in the eyes of the proofreader," Hijiri said. "Did I just say 'equally fair'? Somebody get me a pencil!"

Hijiri laughed. I laughed too.

From there, we talked about a few active projects. I asked for another of the same, and Hijiri ordered herself a real cocktail, made with strawberries.

After a pause, she asked me, "So you don't wear makeup at all? This is you?"

"Pretty much, yeah." Finding myself the topic of conversation, I answered with a little too much force and tried to play it off with a sip of water.

"Nothing? Ever?"

"Not nothing . . . I just don't use much."

"You're not one of those natural types, are you?"

"Natural types?"

"Yeah, you know," she said, "the ones who are all 'natural and proud' or whatever." Hijiri smiled like she was amused, teeth emerging slightly from her shapely lips.

"There are people like that?"

"God yes," she said, then drank whatever was left in her glass and ordered another. "The ones who are all like, oh, I'm so natural, just being the me I'm supposed to be. The ones who are all like, the older I get, the more I'm into who I really am. The ones who think that all the love they give to all things natural means that nature loves them back. The ones who go around telling themselves that everything happens for a reason, and they pat themselves on the back for all their positive energy. The ones who think everything has some kind of hidden meaning . . . Believe me, I can keep going."

I gave a noncommittal response.

"I know, everyone should live their life the way they want, whatever that happens to be."

Resting her chin in her hand, Hijiri wiped a drop from the glass with her finger. Her perfectly straight, long eyelashes cast distinct shadows on the skin under her eyes.

"But if you think about it, that just isn't true. What do you think?" she asked.

"About what?" I asked.

"That kind of thinking, I guess. Spirituality, natural living, all of it. It's all so narrow-minded, you know? To me, it's crazy. I don't care what we're talking about—God, divine providence, nature, some super-energy, the universe . . . Why would any force like that ever get caught up with stupid tiny human beings and their stupid, even tinier human problems?"

I nodded.

"Their so-called spirituality is completely self-serving, designed to make them happy, or make the people around them think they've found some kind of happiness. It's this shallow belief in immediate profit. They go around talking about seeing something big. As if everything they feel, everything they're thinking, is so big, bigger than all of us. That's what they do. They act like they're all big, ready to share their happiness with everyone, when the only happiness they care about is their own. Like, why can't they just keep all that stuff to themselves and leave the rest of us alone? I'm fine, I've had some drinks, but I'm not even close to drunk. I'm like a sponge, I swear."

For a while now, Hijiri had been reaching for her glass at a good pace, but I could see no change whatsoever in her face or in her eyes. If anything, I got the impression that drinking somehow made her even sharper. This was our first time out alone together. That said, I had been out for drinks with Hijiri in a group a couple of times, but I'd never actually seen her drunk.

"What about you?" Hijiri asked me, looking at my drink, about a third of which was left. "You don't drink, or can't drink?"

"I can't, I guess," I said. "I had one drink when I was in college, but it made me feel sick. I haven't had anything to drink since."

"Huh," Hijiri said, adding that maybe she would try the mango too, but wound up ordering a Carlsberg. "A buzz can feel so good, though—if you don't overdo it. It loosens you up, makes everything a little softer. I don't really get drunk or anything, but life without alcohol would be kind of unbearable for me."

"So was tonight . . . that kind of night?" I asked. "I mean, I'm not exactly sure what I mean by, you know, that kind of night . . ."

"Same as any other, I guess." Hijiri scratched the corner of her eye with the round tip of her fingernail. "I'm telling you, though, those people are everywhere."

I hummed to show my interest.

"I mean, when you get together with women our age, it's all they want to talk about. Inner peace, lasting happiness. They can't get enough of it. But I'll speak up about pretty much anything, so I'll say the same thing to them that I was just saying to you. Of course, I'm not going out of my way to step on a landmine. I only say something when they're like, you should get in on this, looking all smug. I mean, when someone says something stupid, don't you want to tell them how stupid they sound? But the thing is, if I do, they look at me with so much pity in their eyes. As if I'm work-obsessed, like I've completely lost track of what matters in life, like I have no idea what it all means. They just look at me like I'm the saddest person they've ever seen. Then they tell me how they used to think like me, until one day everything clicked for them. Like, you know, the universe will tell you when the time is right. And I'm just like, who's going to tell me what? I seriously have no idea what they're talking about."

"But not everybody's like that, right?" I laughed.

"I don't know. Everybody's really into horoscopes and fortunes, aren't they?"

"So, um, do those ever come true?"

"Whether they come true or not isn't the point." Hijiri took a sip of her beer. "They only ever write stuff that people want to hear. All that matters is that you believe this thing is written about you. People just want to read something about themselves. And I get that, I do. Not that I'm gonna spend any money on the stuff. No thanks."

"You're just not interested?" I asked.

"I'm really not," Hijiri answered forcefully. "It has nothing to do with believing or not believing. It's more like . . . I don't want to rely on anything, no matter what it is. Whatever answer's on that paper, I don't want it, unless I get there on my own, using my own head. I'll decide what I'm going to do with my own life."

"You don't want to leave it up to somebody else?"

"Exactly. I'm not the kind of person who likes giving up control." Hijiri laughed. "I'll do it myself, you know? But if you say that to those people, they come back with something like, 'No one can make it through this world on their own, that's not what life's about,' and I know that, obviously. I get that, but that's precisely what makes it so important to do things on your own when you can."

Hijiri grabbed the menu, which was made from a thin piece of metal, and gave it a look.

"Want to get some pickles?"

"Sure," I said. Hijiri asked for the pickle plate and the celery sticks.

"Anyway, it's fine. Everyone should just do whatever they want, myself included. But I can't stand it when you're just talking, then out of nowhere, someone's pushing that stuff on you. It puts me in a real mood. They're all so sure that they're the ones who have seen the light, and it's the only identity they've got, so they can't keep their mouths shut. They're always so loud about it, too, like they need you to see how happy they are. And they walk away feeling great about themselves, because they were generous enough to share the secret to their happiness with everybody. Anyway, they just want to feel superior. It's like some superficial celebrity complex, you know?"

Stirring my straw around the last bit of mango drink at the bottom of my glass, I asked Hijiri if it was kind of like religion. She drank her beer like it was water and nodded a couple of times.

"Isn't that a little unfair to religion?" she asked. "I'm sure there are plenty of worthless religions out there—and people who are looking out for no one but themselves—but still, you have to recognize something kind of sublime in some of it. It's always the common people who end up as the victims, the people hoping against hope. Some of those people actually abandon the material world and everything in it in order to access the realm of the righteous. And you know what? I have to respect that."

"Yeah," I said as I took a bite of celery. A flavor no different from the smell filled my mouth. "You're right about that."

"People like that are on another plane. They're nothing like those other people, the spiritual, 'one-with-nature' people, bent on making their own lives that much easier. Wait, is it okay for me to talk like this? Want me to stop? Am I talking too much?"

Hijiri puckered her lips and looked at me like she was sorry. Even though it was dark, the ambient lighting defined the contours of her plump, shapely lips, which looked so full of life that they could have hopped off her face and walked around at any moment.

"No, not at all," I said, telling the truth. "Seriously . . . I'm just thinking about everything. You've given this some serious thought."

"Not really," Hijiri said in a low voice, looking at her glass. "It's just an old habit of mine. I just say what I'm thinking, no filter. Not all the time, of course. I mean, I'm an adult. I know my way of seeing things won't always click for everyone, as anyone on this planet has to know. When I first started my job, I heard it all—how I lacked charm, how I was confrontational, how I wore people out, how I never listened. But those reactions are so common they're basically a kind of tradition, so when men say that kind of thing, stupid as it is, I can let it go. At this point in life, I know better than to expect anything from men. But I swear the other women at work are just as bad beneath the surface."

Hijiri bit into a stick of celery. It made that crunch that only vegetables can make.

"I forget when it was, but a bunch of us were out drinking when something came up, something that had nothing to do with work. One of the senior guys and I had a difference of opinion, and we kinda got into it. Same as always. He was going way too far with what he was saying, and it was clearly going to have an effect on our work going forward so, you know, I stood my ground. But I'm a pretty good talker myself, and in the end I put him in his place. Things had gotten a little gnarly, so we actually ended up calling it a night. But what can you do, right? That was what I thought. It was obvious that no one had ever stood up to this guy before, and he thought he could get away with it because I'm a woman, but that was exactly why I couldn't let it go. I'm going to have to keep working with this guy. It's up to you to make your own environment, right? Anyway, when we get to the station and everyone's saying goodbye, this woman who started a year after me calls my name and comes running over. I was so sure she was going to say something like thanks for setting that guy straight. It was her comment that had set the whole thing off in the first place, so I guess I was expecting some kind of acknowledgement. But instead, she's like, 'Aren't you scared of people hating you? Every time you do this, it hurts your reputation. The more you fight, the more it's going to hurt you in the end.' Not like I'd been trying to stick up for her, but I really didn't see that coming. I just gave her some vague response, then stared right at her for like five seconds solid."

I laughed.

"It's not like I want people to hate me. I'm just not about to go out of my way to make them like me, either. Being liked is wonderful and all, but that's not what life is about, you know?"

Hijiri asked me if I minded if she had another drink, then

looked over the menu and ordered some other cocktail, not the strawberry. The well-dressed bartender, who had maintained his composure since we sat down, offered a brief reply, then disappeared out back. There were a few more customers than earlier, and the faint sounds of people chatting blended with the music playing in the background. Although I heard the voices and recognized that they were making conversation, I was unable to pick up any hint of what they were discussing, as if the air sucked up the meaning of the words the instant that they came out of their mouths. I almost couldn't tell if they were speaking Japanese.

I couldn't be sure how much Hijiri had had to drink, but her appearance and the way she talked were essentially no different than usual, though maybe she was speaking a little quickly. There was so little difference that I had to wonder if she'd been picking the drinks with the least alcohol. I ordered another mango drink. Hijiri let out a contemplative sigh.

"People act like feminism is a dirty word. As if being a strong, hard-working woman has fallen out of fashion. Not that these people have ever thought about any of that before. They say it's different for me. That not everyone is as strong as I am, that most people are weak or whatever. But that's not it. They aren't weak. They're dull. They don't pick up on things. And I'm not strong. I'm honest. Anyway, who cares what's fashionable? How can anybody go through life thinking about crap like that? This is just my personality—it's who I am."

"Dull . . ." I said in a low voice.

"There are lots of ways to be dull, too," Hijiri said, propping her chin up with her palm. "Some are so disgusting, so brutal, it'll make your skin crawl. The things these people say, the things they think. Sometimes I can't take it. I really can't stand it. Like, with that woman from work, at least she was being honest. Honest all the way down. That makes all the difference to me. If you can live your life like that, hey, go for it. But I can't stand the ones who know better but still act all reserved to save their own skin. All they want is power and recognition. It's all they ever dream about, all they want, and they can never get enough, but they'll look at you like the thought's never even crossed their mind. I mean the ones who go around making absolutely certain they never challenge the men around them, or threaten their sense of superiority. In everything they do, they're careful to make sure they never lose. They act like they don't care, but it's all they live for. You can see it in their eyes. Of course, the second some other girl with the potential to undermine their position—someone like them—shows up, she crushes her like it's nothing. These women are heartless. I've seen it so many times, I'm sick of it. But I guess that's fine, too. It's their life. Still, you know what really bothers me? That they're actually naive enough to think that no one's caught on to their stupid little performance. These women think they're fooling all the men around them, but they're only fooling each other. You know, that whole 'I've got this' mentality. That kind of dullness is too much for me. I hate it. So much."

"I think I know what you mean, at least a little," I said, being honest.

"Once I get going on this one, it's really hard for me to stop."

"It's always been like that?"

"Always."

"Really?" This caught me by surprise. "You work with people like that?"

"I wish they were only at work," Hijiri said, looking straight at me.

I never knew what kind of face to make when she stared at me like that.

"They're all over the place. At school, at the salon, the park, the gynecologist. And at home, of course."

Hijiri spread the water droplets on the counter with her

finger. In the bulging surfaces of the drops, the mood lighting turned to gold and shimmered.

"These women are literally everywhere," Hijiri said after a brief pause. We heard a rush of laughter from the seats behind us. The clinking of glasses was followed by the sound of the door opening and a new group of customers coming in.

"Well," Hijiri chuckled. "They never say anything, but I know they all think there's something seriously wrong with me." This made her burst out laughing. "I really should start seeing a therapist this year."

I probably should have laughed the same way as Hijiri, but couldn't do it so I glanced at the clock on the wall. It had been almost an hour since I'd joined her.

"Hey, should we get going?" Hijiri asked, noticing where I was looking.

"Not yet. We haven't been here that long."

"Sounds good," Hijiri said and sighed. "Sorry to carry on like that. I know it doesn't really matter. Except, well, it matters to me. Hey, we've known each other for a pretty long time now, but I still feel like I don't know anything about you. You'll have to tell me about you next time."

"Me? There's nothing even remotely interesting about me." I shook my head. "What we were just talking about was so much more interesting."

"Hey, if you're good with that kind of stuff, believe me, we could do this every day. We could even get on the phone after this. There's so much more where that came from." Hijiri laughed. "Anyway, tell me something about you."

I understood what she was asking, but I couldn't think of a single thing about me that would be worth sharing. My name is Fuyuko Irie, a freelance proofreader, thirty-four years old. I'll be turning thirty-five in the winter. I live alone. I've been living in the same apartment forever. I was born in Nagano. Out in the country. One of the valleys. I like to go out on a walk once a year on my birthday, Christmas Eve, in the middle of the night. But I was sure that no one else could comprehend what made this fun, and I had never mentioned it to anyone before. I had no friends to talk to on a regular basis. That was it. The full extent of what I could tell her about myself.

"What, you don't like talking about yourself?" Hijiri asked me, sort of teasing.

"It's not that," I said. "There's just nothing to say, really."

"Well, are you seeing somebody?"

"Not . . . right now."

"You broke up?" Hijiri knit her brow and leaned in a little closer. She was practically grinning in my face. The buoyant smell of perfume drifted over from around her neck.

"Uh-huh," I said.

"Huh."

This sort of ended the conversation. The two of us quietly drank the rest of whatever was in our glasses before eventually returning to the topic of work.

We talked about the most recent changes to the dictionary, and where to return reference materials. Hijiri told me that next month she might need to ask me to take on an extra book. She wrote something on a piece of paper, but as she was about to hand it over, she shrugged and said that she'd email me instead. Then she apologized for bringing it up, when we had finally moved away from work-related things. But soon enough, the conversation drifted back to work once more: a minor incident where a proofreader had made an author so incensed that they expressed their objections in the margins of a galley, and, on the other end of the spectrum, a situation where an author with a prickly reputation had sent along an incredibly kind thank-you email, after which they came across as a completely different person. Hijiri laughed and said when she's really busy, she starts second-guessing things that everyone should know, like whether there is actually a Kotto Street in Aoyama. But when she looked it up, and it was there, she felt so reassured. I laughed too and told her that I knew exactly what she meant.

We left the bar and walked as far as the main street, where cars were rushing by.

Hijiri had taken care of the bill. I asked her to let me pay for my share, but she said she wouldn't dream of it, insisting that she'd been the only one of us actually drinking.

She made sure I got a taxi first. I fumbled with the window a few times, but finally got it to roll down. I thanked her for the night and waved goodbye. Hijiri effervesced with happiness and gave me a big smile, thanking me for coming out, and reached out to squeeze my fingertips. The light turned green, and the car began to move. I stroked the tips of my fingers, where Hijiri had squeezed them, as I turned around and watched her getting smaller and smaller.

3

The weather over the May holidays was absolutely unpredictable, and from my first day back I was immediately swamped with work.

The galley that had landed on my desk was a first proof: two separate volumes, each with tons of pages. Every day, I spent no fewer than fifteen hours at my desk. This went on for about three weeks, but I still didn't have the time I needed.

Focusing harder only made the text before my eyes break apart and spill across the page like it was running away, so that I had to grab each piece and pin it back to its proper place. Working through the different items, mindful of their contributions to the text, I inspected each and every element, same as always, as if filtering them individually through a screen. The text itself was not so different from the others, apart from the length, and yet something about it, maybe the unfamiliar content, somehow tripped me up and made me feel like everything was hopeless. I pushed even harder, trying to establish something of a normal pace, but this only backfired. It was a vicious cycle. The motion of my eyes across the text began to slow. The way that things were turning out, I had no choice but to call Hijiri and ask her for three more days. This was the first time that I'd asked for something like this, and she readily consented, but after I hung up my spirit took a nosedive.

The next day, Hijiri called me up, sounding worried.

"How's it going?" she asked.

"Just a little more to go," I said. "Sorry it's taking so long."

"I'm the one who should be sorry for bugging you like this," Hijiri said. "I swear I'm not calling to put pressure on you, but you got off the phone so quickly yesterday that I was wondering if everything was okay. That's all."

"I'll definitely be back on track by tomorrow. I'm kind of struggling."

"Don't worry about it, seriously. Take as long as you want. Well, not literally as long as you want, but . . ." Hijiri laughed. "Really, I can wait, though, so don't worry too much."

By the time I finished what was going to be my last page for the month, the sun was already coming up.

Glancing at the stack of pages on my desk, I heaved a sigh and rested my hands on the paper, then let out one more big sigh. The open dictionaries spread over my desk, the books I never would have checked out unless work had demanded it, marked with countless thin green sticky notes, and the mountains of photocopies taken at the library threatened to collapse at any moment.

I took a moment to set things in their proper places, then sharpened all the pencils, which by now were round at the tips, and stowed them in my pencil case and pencil stand. Then I headed to the shower, where I sat down on the little bathing stool and let my head dangle, remaining in that posture for some time as the steamy water streamed over the base of my neck. My back and hips, so stiff that I was certain they would crack in half if I so much as moved, eventually relaxed, and when I tested out my neck, in awe of what hot water can do, I found a softness that had not been there before.

Once I'd dried my hair, I crawled under the covers and shut my eyes, but an indeterminate pattern, almost like a stain, appeared and disappeared under my eyelids. Counting each one made me feel as though sleep would never come to me, but all of a sudden I fell into a dreamless sleep.

I called Hijiri's office at eleven in the morning.

Because they made it sound like the parcel service might not make it there in time, I offered to head over with the manuscript, as long as that worked for them. Hijiri had yet to make it into work, and it seemed like the woman on the other end was unsure of what to say, but eventually she said they would take me up on the offer. We set up a time, and I hung up.

Though I'd only had four hours of sleep, I woke feeling so light that I might as well have spent all night enjoying a restful sleep. I was that refreshed. I opened the curtains to a day of gorgeous weather. The railings on the balconies of the apartment building down the street, the glossy roof tiles of the houses, the deep green leaves of the cherry trees and the drooping telephone wires trembled in the dazzling sun.

Taking the subway and the Yamanote Line, I arrived at the publisher. The giant building towered so high you couldn't see the top of it, while inside of the lobby, every surface was smooth as could be, so that the sounds of footsteps and of people talking drifted and gathered. The figures of people were reflected in the polished stone floor, as if they were walking across a plane of ice. I waited on a sofa so large that four adults could have sprawled out on the cushions. About five minutes later, the woman I had talked to on the phone came jogging up.

She told me that Ishikawa had taken the day off, but said she'd take the manuscript on her behalf. I reached into my tote bag and took out the thick manuscript and handed it to her. Pulling out a couple of pages to confirm the contents, she thanked me and smiled broadly. Then she bowed and said if anything came up that I could expect to hear from Ishikawa. I bowed just as she had and left the building.

Once I'd handed off the manuscript, my body felt even lighter, and when I took a breath, my nostrils tickled with a smell that mixed the gentle end of spring with the intensity of summer.

Under the clear sky, I directed my attention to this part and then that part of my body, but found no pain whatsoever. Now that I had finished my last big task for the month, a sense of relief swept my lungs each time I cycled through a breath, reaching every corner of my being. There was a power gushing out of me in torrents, a force that made it feel like I could walk like this forever, with no need for a specific goal. What a waste to go back home, I told myself. Why not make the most of it? I could go over to Shinjuku, check out the shops, and wander aimlessly around the city streets. It was a perfect day for it.

This radiant feeling stayed with me as my train rumbled down the tracks, bathed in the fresh sunlight of early summer, but while I was sitting there, with all those smiling people, something took hold of me, steadily dragging down my line of sight, as if the feeling that I'd felt when I left the publisher was being broken down and packed away. Now it was no bigger than a sheet of drawing paper, soon becoming small enough to fit into my palm, but before long, it had shrunk into a scrap too small to know what it was, until it finally was gone, impossible to see, no matter how I squinted.

Shinjuku was overrun with an incredible number of people. Young women carrying shopping bags from different stores, people chatting on their phones and laughing in loud voices, girls who had dark circles around their eyes and looked like dolls. Mothers and fathers holding parasols as they pushed babies in carriages. Standing there inside of that bright noise, I began to feel confused about how one goes about wandering aimlessly. I stood there, watching the flow of people, for a good fifteen minutes before I finally decided to go home.

Over the course of the ten-minute walk to the station, my tote bag filled with packets of free tissues and fliers of discount coupons that appeared before my eyes. I had made it as far as the entrance to the subway, people descending as if being sucked down by the stairs, when I was interrupted by a woman waving a sign and found myself unable to continue.

The chubby woman smiled and asked if I could donate blood today. For some reason, her smiling face reminded me of a head of cabbage split perfectly in two. With her back to the stairs, effectively blocking my way, she asked if I would mind telling her my blood type. I said "Type A." This made her gasp and place a hand over her mouth. Amazing, she said, giving me a smile that would make you think we'd been reunited after years apart. Thrilled, she told me in a high-pitched voice that type A was what they needed most that day. Meanwhile, the sign she was holding said in giant letters that type AB and type O were in highest demand.

This was not the first time I'd been unable to say no to giving blood. Dabbing the sweat from my forehead and neck, I followed her lead, a safe distance behind. Once I'd agreed to donate, she barely said another word until we stepped into the lobby of a building, where she pointed out which elevator I had to take. You want the sixth floor, she said as she pushed the button for me, then walked off with her sign.

Up on the sixth floor, I completed registration and a simple screening, after which they led me to a room that had a row of light pink reclining chairs, where I took a seat and lay down on my back.

Someone in a lab coat worked their way around the room, and when they got to me I watched in a daze as they disinfected my arm. The needle that they pushed into my arm like it was nothing was so thick I almost laughed, and the blood that had been circulating in my arm until that second streamed out of my body, rushing safely into the donation bag, a liquid rich in color that seemed wholly unrelated to me.

Once I finished up, filled out a simple survey, and was in the process of helping myself to a free cup of vegetable juice from the vending machine, I happened to catch a glimpse of my reflection in the window glass.

The image of myself that floated to the surface, tinged with blue against a backdrop of the signs, walls, and windows of the nearby buildings, looked absolutely miserable. Not sad, or tired, but the dictionary definition of a miserable person. This was the woman that I saw in the glass, while an assortment of other objects drifted in and out of the reflection. The space around my head was wild with baby hair or stray hairs that had come free. My shoulders sagged, and the skin around my eyes was sunken. My arms and legs looked stubby while my neck looked long and skinny. The tendons around my collarbone and throat stuck out, and my skin was anything but supple, as if the flesh had been deflated, leaving bizarre diagonal lines on my cheeks. What I saw in the reflection was myself, in a cardigan and faded jeans, at age thirty-four. Just a miserable woman, who couldn't even enjoy herself on a gorgeous day like this, on her own in the city, desperately hugging a bag full to bursting with the kind of things that other people wave off or throw in the trash the first chance they get.

* * *

Over time, with the aid of just one can of beer, drunk slowly, or a single cup of sake, I developed the ability to let go of my usual self.

Whether it's beer or sake, the first sip is delicious. At first, drinking gave me a slight headache, but I was amazed how little time it took to get used to the bitterness and the taste. It always made my hands and feet feel heavy, but it made other parts of me feel light, along with a sensation like the inside of my head was expanding a little. All the different things that I was feeling slipped away without actually disappearing from my mind, and I loosened up, as if a pane of glass had been placed between me and my experience, blurring things. The borders of my being gradually thinned, making me feel as if all kinds of things about me were in fact all kinds of things about somebody else. I stopped looking down. It somehow made things feel like they were actually pretty good.

I started drinking on the nights when I had time between finishing work and going to sleep.

The rainy season came in the middle of June, prompting a solid week of downpours. One positive thing about my apartment was that it had good ventilation. Most of the time I never bothered with the AC, but once the excessive humidity had made the pages of my manuscripts and documents begin to curl, I started running cool air while working.

"God, it's so oppressive," Hijiri said. To prove her point, she collapsed onto the table.

She had met me at a cafe in the area to pick up a manuscript, wearing a white form-fitting shirt with a round collar.

"I can't believe we even publish books when the weather's like this. Who wants to read right now?"

"I know what you mean," I said.

"And as soon as this oppressiveness is over, that's when the real hell begins. July is such a horror show. Do you like summer?"

"It's okay," I said, sipping on my water.

"Do you have somewhere you go every year?" Hijiri took a sip of water too. Her lips left a frosty mark on the transparent glass.

"Not really."

"You don't leave town?"

"I mean, maybe."

"Ever leave the country?"

"Leave the country?" I echoed Hijiri, hastening to add, "I mean . . . I'm not really a fan of flying."

"Sure," she said and shrugged. "That's how it is, right? Works for some people, not for others."

I nodded and drank some of my iced tea.

"Are you going back to Nagano?" she asked.

"I don't know yet," I answered vaguely, dabbing the corners of my mouth with the oshibori.

"It's hot there, too, though," Hijiri said, swirling her straw around her glass. She fished out a shrunken piece of ice and put it in her mouth, crunching it between her teeth.

"I know things are going to be crazy just before the Obon holiday, but we'll have a little bit of wiggle room. You should take it easy. And if you've got time, let's get drinks again! Well, I know you wouldn't drink anything. You'd basically be keeping me company."

"Sounds good to me," I laughed.

"Summer always makes me think about earthworms," Hijiri said a minute later.

"Earthworms?" I asked.

"Yeah. One worm, actually. A big, fleshy one. I can see it in my head. I don't know where it is, but there's this worm, all alone. There's just burnt earth, dry and white, as far as the eye can see. Maybe it's the bottom of a dried-up lake or something. There's no grass or any signs of life, kind of like Mars. Nothing moving anywhere. Just the worm, still clinging to life even though everything else is gone, but then its tail is all . . . wait, they have heads and tails, right?"

"Pretty sure, yeah."

"Anyway, its whole body is burning to a crisp."

"Wow," I said.

"The sun's so close it looks like it's about to crash, burning big and hot just overhead. And the whole place is completely dead, no life anywhere. You can tell. There's no water, either. It's as dry as dry can get. So this last living earthworm, like I said, it's drying up from both ends. Its body is turning white, shriveling up. But it's not dying or anything, just drying out. The worm has no idea what's happening, but it's getting harder to move with every passing second, and there's me, as a kid, looking at the worm. I've got this canteen, and there's a bit of water in it. I think it's there for me to drink, but I've got this water, right? And I want the worm to have it. What if I poured some water on it, what would happen? It's the only thing I can think about, but in that world, it's forbidden. Strictly forbidden. So there's nothing I can do but watch the worm shrivel up. Ever since I was a kid, that's the only thing that comes to mind when I think of summer. Not the ocean, or eating watermelon, or going on vacation . . ."

"You mean you have the same dream every summer?" I asked.

"No, it's not a dream. I don't have dreams like that. It's more like every time somebody says something about summer days when it's too hot to move, or even says the word July, this image appears in my mind, like a print of the same photo. In living color. Who knows, maybe I did have a dream like that when I was little."

I nodded quietly and wiped my mouth with my oshibori.

"But when I bend down, holding my nearly empty canteen behind my back, and get my face real close to the worm, which is almost totally dried up now, I finally see it. The worm's got my face."

Saying this made Hijiri laugh out loud. I did the same, then had a gulp of iced tea. For a while, we just sat there. After a period of silence, Hijiri reached her hands out, palms showing, as if she'd just remembered something. For a second, I wondered what she was doing, but then I put it all together. I grabbed my bag and pulled out the envelope containing the galley and the manuscript and handed it to Hijiri. This book was 600 pages, so heavy that it made my wrists shake, even when I was holding it with both hands. Hijiri hugged it to her chest and shook her head, as if acknowledging the thickness and the weight, then looked at me and laughed.

"It's crazy, right? Who has this much to say to people?"

Outside the cafe, I said goodbye to Hijiri and walked off through the dusk.

After visiting a convenience store for some beer and sake, I stopped in a park not far from my apartment, where I sat down on a warm bench and drank a beer. No one was around, but I could hear the sound of a child crying somewhere in the distance. A minute or so after shamelessly finishing off the first beer, I felt a warm sensation spread over my face. Then I emptied the second can, just like that. Moving on to the sake, I peeled the top off of the cup, careful not to spill any, and started walking as I drank.

When I got home, I was so overwhelmed by everything that I sprawled out on the kitchen floor, just by the entrance, and gazed up at the ceiling. An uneventful, quiet evening, spent on the floor, not even cold.

When I turned my head to the side, I saw a modest stack of magazines in a pile by the trash.

I say magazines, but none of them were magazines that I'd actually bought. They were more like coupon booklets and fliers that had been handed to me on the street. There were other things in the stack too—community bulletins and informational magazines that had been left in my mailbox—all of them waiting there until I could put them out on trash day.

Face up on the floor, I looked at the various items in the stack. So many businesses offering so many services, explaining what they had to sell. Sometimes a photo of a smiling employee. Prices and discounts. Salons. Tiny boxes crammed with row after row of tiny text. The benefits of beauty treatments. The specialties of new dentists and doctors. Advice on allergies and Chinese medicine. Address after address.

In ten minutes of reading, I found seven errors and marked each one with my fingernail. At the very bottom of the stack, there was a substantial booklet made with good-quality paper. With a cheek pressed against the floor, I opened the booklet with one hand and flipped through a few pages. It was a cata-log for a place that called itself a culture center, jointly oper-ated by some corporation and a university.

Wondering where I'd gotten it, I flipped from one page to the next and realized that maybe I had wound up with it when I gave blood in Shinjuku. When I had another look at the cover, I saw the words "Course Catalog." They noted that they offered classes at more than a dozen locations nationwide, this booklet being for the Shinjuku campus. Even a quick look revealed information on a truly staggering number of classes. There was every kind of intellectual activity or hobby you could think of, filling page after page. I sat up, taking the cat-alog in my hands, and gave it a careful read.

Glancing at the table of contents, I found that the classes were divided into broad categories like foreign languages, community engagement, the arts, and lifestyle, and subdivided into more specific topics, an average of ten classes or so for each.

Every category had a fair share of elementary-sounding titles like "An Introduction to Greek Politics," "Reading Soseki," and "Opera for Beginners," surveys of iconic books and cultures from across history and the globe, but skipping ahead I encoun-tered a number of courses that were not immediately clear to me, such as "Gnosis and Kukai," "The Vimalakirti Sutra and the Book of Revelation," "The Special Theory of Relativity and Space-Time Distortion," and "Understanding Insects," along with others like "Love, Spirits and Channeling," "Moxibustion Now," "Mysteries of the Wani," and "Enjoying Kuzushiji and Zen," each of which I carefully examined.

There were also classes in braille transcription and sign language, as well as translation and conversation classes for the major foreign languages, along with languages like Swedish, Slovak, and Hindi, classes on everything from writ-ing essays to baking bread, watercolor painting and ink-wash painting, tsurushi kazari, bisque dolls, photography, calligraphy, dance and gagaku, tango and chanson, weaving, sculpture, gardening, bobbin lace, all about Buddhist statues, woodworking and the way of tea, tai chi, and tropical fish, not to mention a variety of classes taught in the field, throughout Japan as well as internationally, where you could sample sushi at Tsukiji or go on tours of old castles and Romanesque cathedrals . . . there was such a wide selection of options that before I knew it I'd spent two whole hours reading through the course titles and instructor names and summaries. Since the courses weren't numbered, I wasn't able to figure out the exact total, but I'd guess there were almost a thousand courses in the catalog. Apart from a few spelling inconsistencies, I came across no misprints.

I was positively baffled by the idea that enough experts were out there in the world for them to offer classes in this many areas of expertise, or culture, or education, or whatever you might call it, and on top of that enough interested people, at least ten or twenty times the number of instructors, to make the courses viable, and for a while I lay motionless, sprawled out on the kitchen floor. When I imagined classes like this being held, day in and day out, inside a building somewhere in Shinjuku, it was almost too much for me to take, and a sigh came rolling out of me.

I grabbed another cup of sake from the fridge and lay back down on the floor, holding my head up enough to drink it. Musing over the way sake looks essentially the same as water but tastes completely different, I closed my eyes and let myself enjoy the feeling of my body loosening up. Once I'd peeled off my socks and jeans, I started feeling silly and laughed out loud. Hahaha. As soon as I did, I could see the sounds before my eyes. When I said hahaha, I could see hahaha, when I said teehee I could see teehee. Realizing this made me laugh even harder. Then when I was done, the silence was so funny that I started laughing again. Rolling my head around on the floor as I laughed, I could feel all the bumps and dents of my skull, making me aware of just how different the two sides of my head were. I raised my head as high as my neck would allow, then let everything go all at once, making a dull fat thud, which was so physically enjoyable that I did it again, over and over. This eventually made me nauseous, and that feeling was joined by a drowsiness that started to fill the space behind my eyes and my forehead, and before I knew it I had fallen into a deep sleep.

4

It could have been because it was a Sunday, or maybe it was always this way, but the main hall of the culture center was teeming with people.

Most of them looked like well-dressed housewives, but there were also some students and people who could have been retirees. Some of them had to be friends or at least know each other. They sat together on white sofas set up along the walls or in the chairs arranged around the tables, making small talk or exchanging quick hellos. My ears made room for all the pleasant sounds around me. It was like being in a hospital lobby. There were no patients with bandaged limbs or doctors in white coats, and there was just a little more laughter, and a different smell, but the scene felt very similar to me.

The classes that required a year-round commitment felt like a reach, so I looked through the one-off classes, but there was nothing that felt like a perfect fit, and I began to feel unsure of what I was doing. For the past couple of weeks, I had been washing away this feeling by heading to the kitchen for a beer. Eventually, I decided it was best for me to go and see the culture center for myself, to get an idea of what kind of place it was.

Carrying my wallet, phone, and a thermos full of cold sake in a tote bag slung over my shoulder, I sailed around the lobby. The entire back wall of the space had been outfitted with shelves, filled with innumerable cream-colored leaflets on the courses being offered. The leaflets were more detailed than the catalog, providing more information about the courses, along with bios and photos of the instructors. There were even some courses not listed in the catalog.

The most I had been able to decide was that I wanted to study something completely new to me, something I knew nothing about. I picked out a few options that would fit my schedule and budget. As a rule, I stayed away from any classes where the group gets up and moves around, or where you had to make something or share your work with everybody. The classes I flagged were all a bit more conventional, where you sat down and listened to someone lecture.

After several trips up and down the wall of tightly packed shelves, I'd collected leaflets for five classes: "An Invitation to Byzantine Art," "Global Tragedy Traditions," "The Fascinating Lives of Marine Mammals," "The Funeral and Zen," and "Dependency and the Nation." I took a seat on one of the sofas and told myself it was time to make a decision. Pick one now. The place was crowded, but it was bright. The atmosphere was nice, and I didn't hate being there. Does it even matter what you pick? Stop overthinking things. Just pick one like you're drinking a beer. Stop worrying. Let go and have some fun. Sure, it could be a waste of money, but you can always leave.

I went into the bathroom, where I pulled out my thermos and had cup after cup of sake, but sitting on the toilet seat for so long was making me a little sleepy, so I went out to the vending machines in the hallway and bought a can of black coffee, which I drank on the spot. Then I made up my mind: "Global Tragedy Traditions"! Feeling a burst of courage, I threw the empty can into the recyclables. It landed with a goofy clang.

To take care of registration, I walked up to the nearest service counter. A woman wearing glasses with thin silver frames eyed the ticket machine just behind me. Embarrassed to have missed this, I bowed and walked off. A middle-aged woman waiting for her turn gave me a nasty look, then quickly turned away. The electronic display above the counter gave the current number as 340. I was 357. I went back to the same sofa as before and waited for my number to be called.

It took longer than I thought it would. After lunch, the crowd swelled to an even greater size. In something of a daze, I reminded myself that it probably only got this crowded on Sundays. With my tote bag in my lap, I closed my eyes and waited.

Though unsure of whether it was coming from my head, stomach, or lower back, I felt something disgusting swirling inside of me, a clear reminder of the nauseated feeling I experienced the first time I ever drank—fourteen years earlier. But I was in no position to go home. Nope. I had to stick it out at least until I finished registration. I leaned against the wall and grasped the fabric of the tote bag, lumped in my lap between my hands. Eventually the feelings subsided, but when I heard my number and stood up, I felt sure I was going to throw up. Stopping mid-stride, I swallowed several mouthfuls of saliva before proceeding to the counter, but the next thing I knew the nausea had returned. I waved to the receptionist to hold on for a moment. Glancing back, I saw a sign that had an arrow pointing to the bathroom, so I pointed at the sign, hoping she would understand, then shuffled over to the bathroom with my hand over my mouth. But then my stomach rumbled strangely and began to spasm. I felt the root of my tongue in the back of my throat go tense and the contents of my stomach travel upward. The bathroom was at the far end of the hall, as far away from registration as possible. I closed off my throat with my tongue, clenching my teeth as I tried desperately to stop the liquid from reaching my mouth, but I didn't make it in time.

At the entrance to the bathrooms, I vomited into my hands,

rivulets of brownish liquid dribbling between my fingers. As soon as I took a deep breath, I felt like I was going to throw up again, and I did, into my palms. At that moment, somebody exited the men's room and we ran into each other. Apparently failing to notice my vomit or the fact that I was throwing up, he tried stepping around me and lost his balance. A girl on her way out of the women's room asked me if I was okay and led me inside. I washed my hands at the sink, nodding over and over, then rinsed my mouth out and apologized to the girl. I'm sorry, I'm fine, I'm so sorry. The girl handed me a folded mass of paper towels. She watched me through the mirror for a second, like she had her doubts, but finally she winced a little and said okay, bowing as she left.

I sat down in the same stall as before, hanging my head and waiting for the feeling to pass. Much better for having thrown up, I took deep breaths over and over as I rubbed my stomach.

I gave myself some time, but I didn't get the sense that I was going to throw up again, so I left the stall and went to look at the entrance. I was relieved to see that the vomit had been confined to the tiles, narrowly missing the carpet. Working with a bucket and a blackened, beat-up rag that I borrowed from the broom closet, telling myself I could replace it later I mopped up every bit of vomit I could find. Once I'd finished wringing out the rag, I wanted to give up on everything and go straight home, but I realized that I'd left my tote bag at the registration area.

The main hall was the same as it had been, full of people chatting and reading leaflets and fliers waiting for their turn to register. From a safe distance, I looked toward the counter, but saw no sign of my bag. The person registering at the counter finished up, and before the next number was called, I seized the opportunity and started saying something to the woman, but she cut me off mid-sentence and asked if I would please take a number, so I did, then went back to the sofa to wait, just like before. At this point there were six people ahead of me.

Looking around the lobby, watching nothing in particular, I realized that the man seated on the sofa diagonally across from me had been looking my way periodically for some time now. Since nobody was sitting on either side of me, there was a good chance that he was actually looking at me. I pulled a handkerchief from my pocket and nonchalantly wiped the area around my mouth. To my relief, there was no trace of anything on my handkerchief.

A few minutes later, the man was still looking at me, which made it hard for me to stay calm. I had no idea where I should look and was beginning to feel helpless when it hit me. What if he was the man I bumped into by the bathroom, when I threw up?

I casually glanced at his shoes. Because of the angle, I could only see the sole of one of them, but it appeared clean, as was his pant leg. It seemed unthinkable that I could have gotten his hands and face, but it was possible that I'd gotten some part of him, somewhere I couldn't see from where I was sitting. That being the case, I figured the best thing to do was go up and apologize to him. But what was I supposed to do if he was actually someone else?

My heart was burdened by a leaden darkness, but I took one breath after another, telling myself that this was my responsibility. Just think of it as work and you'll do fine. I stood up decisively and walked over to where he was sitting.

This was the first time in my life that I had said something to an unfamiliar person in an unfamiliar place.

"Excuse me," I said, looking at his chin. ". . . A little while ago, over by the bathrooms, did you get . . ."

Stopping there made it impossible to pick up the sentence where I left off. I was so nervous I became unsure of what I should have said next. Did you get my . . . Did I get your . . . I did my best to form a proper sentence in my head, but I wasn't able to do much more than stutter. Then he spoke.

"I thought it was you. From earlier. Is everything okay?"

"I'm okay," I said, swallowing my saliva. The man said he was glad to hear it and smiled slightly, after which a silence took over.

There was some gray mixed with his black hair, which had receded a good distance from his forehead and shot off here and there in little curls. His eyebrows, neither thick nor thin, were flecked with white hair too, drooping down like an open bridge. Though it was hard to tell his age, he looked like he was probably in his fifties. He had on a dark blue polo shirt, faded and worn out, with a few different pens in the pocket at his chest. He was wearing worn-out light beige cotton slacks and a pair of sneakers, though it was hard to tell at first if they were leather or plastic.

"So, um," I said, breaking the silence. "About earlier . . . I wasn't really . . . I'm sorry I didn't apologize, but, um, I was worried that maybe I got some on your shoes." It was a struggle to get the words out, but at least this time I had finished the thought.

"Oh," he laughed, glancing at his shoes. "Nothing to worry about. And it's my fault for not watching where I was going. I'm the one who should apologize."

"No, it's my fault," I said back.

There really wasn't anything to say after that. I bowed and backed away. He bowed too. I started heading back to the sofa, but they called my number before I got there, so I changed course and headed for the counter.

"Excuse me, but I think I left a tote bag over here." I placed the tiny slip of paper with my number on the counter.

The woman with silver frames looked at me, spun around in her chair, then spun back around holding my dark blue bag and plopped it on the counter.

"Thank you," I said as I bowed. Without responding, the

woman at the counter swept her hair behind her ear as she called the next number, clearly out of patience.

I threw the bag over my shoulder and headed for the exit, but I couldn't stop myself from looking over at the man. His legs were crossed, he had some kind of notebook in his lap, and he was hunched over writing something. I walked slowly down the hallway to the elevators and pressed the button. When the elevator came, I stepped in, went downstairs and left the building.

The afternoon sun came up like a flood and made me squint. The plaza just outside the building looked like a sea without water, while the hands on the clock, standing like a sword thrust in the ground, pointed to three on the dot.

The next Sunday, I went back to the culture center in Shinjuku carrying a replacement for the rag.

I put it in my tote bag, along with my wallet and a thermos of sake. I was downstairs and outside before I realized I'd forgotten my phone, but decided to leave it. No one ever called me unless it was for work, and it was a Sunday. I walked to the station, pushing through the heavy, humid air.

I had been drinking since eight in the morning, four cans of beer to be precise. I had done some experimenting since what happened at the culture center, and I'd discovered that I wouldn't get sick as long as I didn't mix alcohol with caffeine, so I drank only beer in the morning.

The main hall had not changed in the slightest from the week before. It was almost like the intervening time had contracted, and I had been standing there only a few hours earlier.

Thanks to the beers I'd had at home and the sake that I drank on a bench at the station while I was waiting for the train, I was feeling pretty loose, though not in a good way. I was out of it, wondering if maybe I'd had too much, but I started to feel like none of that mattered anyway, it was going to be fine. I took my ticket and sat down on the sofa, then took a long look at the numbers on the ticket. According to the digital display, I would have to wait for thirteen people to be called before it was my turn.

Sitting on the edge of the sofa, I slumped so far back that I was practically lying down and watched the people moving around the room and chatting like they were having a great time. There was an area close to where I was sitting that had been turned into a cafe, with partitions short enough that I could see the tops of people's heads as they relaxed and drank their tea. Different heads of different colors. There were also lots of people seated in the chairs lined up along the entryway by the register, waiting for seats. The sounds of cutlery blended with the smell of coffee on a stream of air that drifted over to my face.

My fingers were heavy and my elbows were jelly. I took the thermos out of the tote bag in my lap, unscrewed the cap, then poured myself a cup and drank it in one gulp. It went down slow and warm. Pretty soon I sensed that unmistakable smell working its way back up. I glanced at the showcase full of cheesecakes and locked eyes with a man on his way out of the cafe area. It was the man from last week.

He looked at me and smiled gently, nodding hello. Though confused about why he was smiling, I followed along and nodded back.

"Are you here for a class?" the man asked with a cheerful expression.

I nodded several times, then told him I was waiting. It had been a week since I'd said sorry to this person, but I felt like everything had happened minutes earlier.

"What are you waiting for?" he asked. The chest pocket of that faded dark blue polo bristled with mechanical pencils and regular pencils, bulging outward to an absurd degree that captured my attention.

For some reason, the man just stood there, without moving, staring at me. Then I realized that he had asked me something, so I carefully rewound the conversation in my head and gave him an answer. "I'm waiting to be called." I felt the sake reach the bottom of my stomach. "I'm waiting to be called," I said again. The air I'd just swallowed was now threatening to resurface, so I swallowed my saliva in an attempt to keep it down.

"Oh, okay," the man said, glancing back toward the counter.

"That—" I pointed at his chest pocket. "Could be dangerous, if you fell."

"What could?" the man asked, opening his eyes a little wider.

"Your pocket," I said, my finger still in midair.

"My pocket could be dangerous?"

"The pens. You could get hurt. If you fell. Your throat."

The man jutted out his neck and looked at his chest pocket, then looked back at me.

"The sharp ends are pointing down, so I'll be fine. The tops are round."

"Oh," I said and let out a huge sigh. "So being round makes them safe, huh?"

"I think so, yes."

"That's a leaf."

"Sorry?"

"Relief . . . I said *that's a relief*."

After letting out a succession of huffs, as if I had become the smokestack of some kind of a machine, I took a giant breath and let the whole thing out.

With every breath, my arms and legs got heavier, draining the energy from my body without actually making me sleepy, but my eyelids started to fall shut.

I rubbed my eyes, at this point basically lying down. No amount of concentration could prevent my eyelids from lowering, so I used my index fingers to pull up the skin around my eyebrows.

"Um," the man said. "It looks like you've had something to drink."

"Yeah," I said.

"Are you going to class drunk?" the man asked, leaning forward slightly.

"No, I'm not," I said. "I just came to put the rag."

"Put the rag?"

"To make up for . . . the bathroom."

"Did you break something?"

"For the bathroom," I said, pointing in the direction of the bathrooms.

The man nodded understandingly at my words. Before I knew it, he had left my field of vision. I set aside the tote bag I was hugging and crossed my arms, no longer able to resist the force of my eyelids. Before long, I fell asleep.

A buzzing sound circled around me, working its way closer from somewhere in the distance, until finally it was right in front of me and made me open my eyes wide, no idea what time it was or where I was. I felt something cold below my tongue, around my chin, so I wiped it off with the back of my hand. It was drool.

One glance around the main hall showed that nothing had changed: people were chatting with each other, waiting for their numbers to be called, sitting in chairs and reading. Looking up at the clock on the wall, I saw it was three-thirty. Apparently I'd been sleeping here for about three hours. I rubbed my eyes with the backs of my hands and tentatively shook my head, which was filling with a splotchy haze.

I was clueless as to what to do with myself now, no idea where I should go or what to do once I stood up, which meant that I sat in the same position I had woken up in for another twenty minutes. Then a melody played and made me jump. My shoulders practically touched my ears. The melody echoed through the hall, louder with every repetition. Just as I was wondering how loud it would get, it stopped. The doors beyond the counter opened, and out poured a succession of people buzzing in conversation. Among the faces and heads, I saw the man in the dark blue polo shirt, who nodded at me and walked over.

He stood right in front of me, where I sat on the sofa, so that I had to lift my eyes to look at him. From his bag, he pulled out a plastic bottle of water, which he held out for me.

"I got this for you earlier, but when I came back you were sleeping. Here," he said.

"Earlier?" I asked. My voice was a little hoarse. "You mean like three hours ago?"

"Yeah. I had class. I just got out, and you were still here, so here we are."

When the man smiled, stark wrinkles appeared in his cheeks and at the corners of his eyes, which somehow made me feel terribly embarrassed about everything. Looking down, I bowed and told him that I was sorry.

"You were just sleeping, there's no need to apologize," he laughed. "The other day, it looked like you weren't feeling very well. I was worried that might be the case again today. If you tell someone at the desk, they have a place in the back where you can lie down for a while."

"Um, I think I'm okay now, though," I said, nodding several times, and bowed again. "Sorry for bothering you."

"Here," said the man, offering me the bottle again. I pressed one hand against my forehead and hesitantly took the bottle with the other. I was so thirsty, but for some reason, I wasn't able to unscrew the cap, bring the water to my lips, and take a drink in front of him. Holding the bottle up, I said thank you and bowed again. But when I looked over to my other hand, resting on the sofa, I noticed that my tote bag was gone.

* * *

". . . Okay. If it turns up, we'll call you at this number."

The young police officer read through the incident report, then took a quick glance at my face.

He had a strange way of speaking, devoid of any emotion. I thanked him for his time, bowed, and left the precinct. I'd looked all around for the bag, with the help of the staff at the culture center, but we never found it.

"I'm sorry," I told the man from the culture center, who had come with me and waited for me outside while I filled out the report. I bowed. "It's my fault for not paying more attention."

"Far from it," the man said. "I just hope they can find it."

"I feel bad. You spent your whole afternoon chasing it with me . . . and even came all the way here."

"At least you didn't have your phone or any credit cards in there, anything you'd have to call and have them stop. Wait, what about your ATM card?" he asked.

"Oh, it's at home."

"That's good. Sometimes wallets show up later, but empty."

"Really?"

"Sure. They'll take the cash, then toss the rest. I'm always losing things, but I've gotten my wallet back twice."

"Really?"

"Hopefully there's something in there with your address on it," he said.

The man and I walked down the street, heading toward the subway at Shinjuku Station.

Neither of us said a word the whole way there. As I watched

the tips of my sneakers stepping forward on the dirty asphalt and flagstones, I realized how unnatural and unsettling it made me feel to walk empty-handed through an unfamiliar section of the massive city.

At the station, just before the ticket gate, as people rushed around us, I expressed my gratitude to the man.

"Thank you for being so kind today."

Since I had lost my money when I lost my wallet, I wound up borrowing a thousand yen.

"Is that enough?" he asked.

"It is, thanks." I bowed. "I'll pay you back, right away."

"Take your time. I'll be there next week, too. If you see me, please say hello."

I'll be there next week, too. When he said these words, everything that had happened at the sofas and the counter and the bathrooms replayed inside my head, leaving me depressed. I hesitated until the last possible second, but I finally asked him for a way to get in touch, just in case. He happily agreed, so I borrowed something to write with. We wrote our information down and swapped.

"San . . . taba?" I asked, trying to decipher the characters in the name that he had written on the slip of paper.

"Mitsutsuka," he said with a laugh.

"Mitsutsuka," I said.

"Right."

"Mitsutsuka," I said again.

"But I get Santaba all the time. Sanzoku, too." Smiling, he adjusted the position of his brown shoulder bag. "And you're Fuyuko Irie."

"Right," I replied, though something about him saying my whole name to my face made it impossible for me to look directly at him, so I looked down at the tips of Mitsutsuka's shoes.

"See you," Mitsutsuka said and gave me a short wave,

disappearing into a fresh crowd of people seconds after passing through the gate.

* * *

"Losing your wallet is a special kind of devastation, isn't it?"

Hijiri sighed loudly into the receiver.

"Did you have them stop your cards?" she asked.

"Yeah," I said before I had a chance to think. I didn't actually have any credit cards for them to stop. At this point it had been four days since I lost my bag, but there had been no word from the police.

"Well, at least you have your phone, that's something to be grateful for."

"Yeah," I said.

"You didn't notice anything?" Hijiri asked. Not mentioning the fact that I was so drunk that I'd fallen asleep, I explained that I was sort of lost in thought, sitting there on the sofa, and the next thing I knew the bag was gone.

"People are always walking off with bags."

"Yeah."

"But if someone's taking it, they're taking it. It's not like being careful is going to change anything."

"True."

"It all comes down to luck, I guess."

"Yeah."

"As awful as it was to have somebody steal your stuff, at least you had that nice guy there to help." Hijiri could hardly believe it. "Maybe that's its own form of balance, huh?"

"I guess so," I said.

"What were you doing at a place like that, anyway?" Hijiri asked, circling back. "Are you taking a class there?"

"I was just running an errand, for a friend."

"Oh, okay."

The tone of her voice suggested that my lie was working.

"Those places have an interesting take on culture," Hijiri laughed. "And the nice man, he was at the culture center, too?"

I gave her a vague answer. Hijiri hummed, still skeptical. From there, we talked about the usual work stuff for a while before hanging up.

The day after I lost my bag, I called Mitsutsuka at the number he had written down for me (after having two cans of beer), to work out a time for me to pay him back.

I had considered sending him cash by registered mail, but he'd told me that he worked pretty close to where I lived, so we decided to meet up the next evening at a cafe right outside a station I'd never used before, basically the halfway point between us. After we decided on a time and a place and hung up, I felt uneasy, like I was making a mistake, but once I'd had one or two more beers, the alcohol eclipsed all of the questions in my head, pushing them out of view.

On the day I promised to meet Mitsutsuka, I devoted the whole morning to diligently reviewing the work that I had done the day before, then made myself some lunch and took a quick break. After that, I headed to the local library to return some books, then worked until six, checking a handwritten manuscript against its galley.

As the time of our meeting approached, I grew more and more uneasy, glancing at the clock over and over, but every time I did, I sighed.

Once the hands of the clock pointed to ten after six, I organized the manuscripts and galley pages spread across my desk and sharpened all my pencils to a perfect point and stood them in the pencil stand, then washed my face, put on some moisturizer, and brushed my hair. I went back and forth about putting my hair up, but in the end I left it down. Then I went into the kitchen, opened the fridge, and took out a beer, which I drank slowly before going back into my room.

Looking through my dresser drawers, I thought a lot about what I should wear, not that I had much of a choice, so I went with the freshly washed t-shirt sitting folded on the very top and a pair of cotton slacks. Now that I was dressed, I stood in front of the full-length mirror by the door and looked at myself for the first time in a while and scanned myself from head to toe. When I turned to the side, I had the peculiar sensation of finding myself far skinnier than I remembered, and for a while I just stared into the mirror. Then I faced forward and tried to stare into my own eyes, which I found staring back at me. Mottled with shadows, my face stared back at me with the most uncertain expression. If only those parted lips would tell me something, I knew that I would listen to them, whatever they might have to say, but no matter how I waited, no words came from anywhere. I became unsure of how to leave the mirror, how to leave the me in the mirror behind. I rested my hands on the top of my head. Then following the contours of my skull, I brought them slowly downward. Once I had made it from my temples to my cheeks, I brought them up to the top and slid my palms down again, top to bottom. The me inside the mirror repeated the same movements. I did the same thing over and over again, until it was time for me to leave the house.

Through the window of the cafe, I could see that Mitsutsuka had arrived ahead of me and was reading a book. Feeling the beers that I'd had earlier, especially in my cheeks, I pushed on the door, went inside, and sat down across from Mitsutsuka, saying sorry, then pulled an envelope containing a thousand-yen note out of my bag and placed it on the table and bowed as I slid it over. I could see that one of the corners had been bent, even though I'd put the envelope inside my note-book to protect it.

"Thank you so much for your help."

"No problem," I heard him say, watching his hand rest on the envelope. A brief silence followed, but I couldn't bring myself to look him in the eye, instead awkwardly dabbing my cheeks with my handkerchief or gathering my bag into a ball.

"Sorry to make you go out of your way," Mitsutsuka said, breaking the silence, to which I shook my head over and over.

"It didn't need to be this week. It could have waited until the next time you came to the culture center."

"Thanks," I said. My mouth was sticky and dry, so I took a sip from the glass of water on the table. "But I don't think I'm going to the culture center anymore."

"Is that right?" Mitsutsuka asked.

I nodded a few times, my hands on the tote bag in my lap.

"You're finished with your class?"

"No," I said. "I had been thinking about signing up, but it looks like it isn't going to work out."

"I see," Mitsutsuka said, nodding affirmatively.

Another silence ensued, much like the last, during which I scratched the skin around my eyebrow with my fingertip, then looked down, making my hair fall into my face. I put my hair behind my ears, but then I started worrying about how I should be sitting. I stared at the surface of the table for a while. It had been wiped down, without leaving any drips or streaks to speak of, but it was clear that no amount of wiping would undo the stubborn layers of grime that had accumulated. I wanted something to drink, beer or sake. My thoughts went to the silver thermos I had lost. The mild buzz that I had been feeling when I made it to the station, and up until I stepped into the cafe, was for whatever reason fading quickly, which made me feel alone. At this point, something occurred to me. I had returned the money I had borrowed, satisfying the objective of our meeting.

Surely the most reasonable thing to do would be to get up now and leave. Pretty soon I couldn't bear the thought of sitting there any longer. Glancing at Mitsutsuka, I thought his face betrayed an air of awkwardness as well. And then it hit me: maybe he was waiting for me to get up and leave him alone, and once I started thinking that I couldn't stop. I took a deep breath and pushed back my chair to get up. That's when Mitsutsuka spoke.

"What would you like?"

Of course. We hadn't ordered anything. Looking at the menu, I pointed at the first two words I saw and said that I was having a hot coffee. I could tell that I was red in the face.

Mitsutsuka said he would have the same. A middle-aged lady made her way over to our table from the back and set a glass of water down in front of me, then took our order. Wearing a black apron wrapped around a figure so full and round that she was a sight to behold, the woman acknowledged our requests with no more than a subtle movement of the chin, not uttering a word. Then moving just as slowly as when she'd come over, she made her way out back again. Her arms and legs seemed far too skinny for the rest of her. This is when I realized that the water I had sipped just after sitting down had belonged to Mitsutsuka, and blushed as I silently swapped the new glass with the one I had drunk from earlier.

We waited for our coffee to arrive, without saying a word.

"Do you work somewhere around here?" I finally asked, unable to take the indescribable silence. Scavenging what little I could gather of my buzz, if there was any left at all, I cautiously attempted to make conversation.

"I do," Mitsutsuka said. "At a high school, by the station."

"So, you're a teacher?" I asked.

"Yes."

"You're a teacher," I said, nodding as I wiped my mouth with my handkerchief. "What do you teach?"

"I teach physics," Mitsutsuka said.

"Physics?"

"That's right."

"So when you say physics . . ." I said, but was unable to continue. The lady made her way back to the table and set our coffee down, turning the handles of the cups to three o'clock. We solemnly observed her series of movements, as if witnessing some kind of a ceremony. She pinched the lip of the small platter with the sugar and cream and dragged it to the middle of the table, then placed the bill by the edge before walking off again.

Mitsutsuka took a sip of his coffee.

"What about you, Ms. Irie?" he asked. "Are you employed?"

Being called by my name made me tense. I thought that I might have some of my coffee, but it was so black and hot that I opted for some water instead. "Um, I work at home."

"At home."

"Right . . . I'm a proofreader, but I work from home, freelance."

"So you proofread books?"

"Right."

"Wow," Mitsutsuka said, his eyes discernibly wider. "A proofreader?"

"Yeah."

"What kind of books do you work on?"

"Nothing too technical, but I can do pretty much anything else."

"Even novels?"

"Yeah."

"Really?"

"Yeah."

"Is it hard?" he asked.

"The work, you mean?"

"Yes."

"I don't know . . . Maybe, because I'm sitting the whole time, but that isn't exactly hard. I guess it's not that hard, not really."

"Huh."

". . . So, Mr. Mitsutsuka, what grade do you teach?"

"All grades," he said. "Of course, it's just a normal high school, so no one ever has a serious interest in physics."

"Really?"

"Sadly, no," he said, then brought his cup to his lips and took a gulp, tilting his head back just a little.

"Isn't that hot?" I asked in disbelief.

"It is," Mitsutsuka said. "I don't know why, but I can drink boiling hot drinks like they're room temperature."

"Wow."

From there, working through lengthy stretches of silence, we spoke a little about the culture center, where we had met. I thought that maybe Mitsutsuka taught some kind of class for them, but that apparently wasn't the case. He was there as a student.

"As a proofreader, you're reading all the time, so you must learn a lot about all kinds of things," Mitsutsuka said after a while.

I nodded vaguely. "I guess so . . . but proofreading isn't anything like reading . . . It's completely different," I said, the hand gripping the handkerchief resting in my lap.

"That makes sense," Mitsutsuka said, nodding as he took another sip of coffee.

"The first thing they teach you as a proofreader is that you're not supposed to read the story on the page. That goes for a novel or any other kind of book. No reading allowed."

"You're not supposed to read?"

"Right. As a proofreader, no matter what you're working on, you're not allowed to get lost in the text."

Mitsutsuka nodded.

". . . The goal is to read as little as possible . . . Of course, we're proofreading, so we have to engage with every aspect of the story. Plot, continuity, chronology, everything. Anyway, the idea is to keep our emotions out of it . . . to focus our energy on finding all the errors hiding in the book."

"Honestly, that sounds pretty difficult to me," Mitsutsuka said.

"Novels can be pretty difficult, I guess. They're kind of made to act on your emotions, and sometimes that can suck you in. When I was just getting started, I had no clue where or how to read with an eye for mistakes."

"So that's something you figure out with training?"

"Yeah. At least that's what they say, but I think it's true that some people are cut out for it and others aren't."

"What makes someone good at it?"

"Well . . . you're sitting at your desk, not moving all day long, looking for mistakes, so if you're the kind of person who wants to get up and move around, it might be a lot."

"A good fit for someone who can put up with all the sitting."

"Also, you're pretty much always working on your own, so I guess you have to be the kind of person who doesn't mind being alone—who isn't bothered by it."

"That makes sense."

"Yeah."

"And it's been working out for you?"

"I never really liked reading. Or more like I never read much, really. I didn't really have those emotions . . . Well, maybe not emotions. Maybe sensitivity? Whatever it is, I didn't have much of it, which made it easy to get used to," I said.

I took a sip of coffee. It was a little cooler now.

"In a way," I said, "maybe it was a good fit for me. As soon as I finish a book, I forget the story and whatever facts were in it. I forget it, all of it. Sometimes all I can remember is the title. After a couple of years, it's pretty much gone. When I read, it's like I'm not actually reading, and when I'm done reading, I never feel like I can say I've actually read the thing. It's always the same. By the time I start on the next manuscript, my mind's blank and I can start fresh, looking for mistakes. That's why no matter how long I do this, I'll never be a walking encyclopedia. Nothing sticks."

After saying all that in one breath, I thought that I might still be a little drunk after all. Looking down at my hand gripping the handkerchief, I saw that my fingertips were trembling.

For a minute or so, we drank our coffee, neither of us breaking the silence.

Outside the window, the layers of twilight spread across the sky were being steadily eroded by the night, from which emerged the bright faces of the students, chatting as they walked, a bicycle speeding up now and then to pass them, bells ringing when their paths crossed. With my lips pressed to my cup, I gazed into the thickness of the night, an inky substance that filled the space between that which moved and that which did not.

"Do you like reading?" I asked.

"I almost never read anymore, but there was a time when I liked reading books."

"Mostly novels?"

"For the most part. They did nothing for my studies, but I loved reading novels in my student days. I feel like I read nothing but the old ones. I know I read a lot of them, too, but now I can't recall what any of them were about . . . Maybe all of us forget, not just the proofreaders." Mitsutsuka smiled. Whenever he smiled, two big wrinkles pushed the other ones aside, making his gentle face look even more relaxed, and I couldn't help but smile too. Lines formed across his forehead, which he rubbed with the flat of his palm, until his coffee reclaimed his attention, and he took another gulp. I glanced down at the pens in the front pocket of his shirt, then pressed my lips together, looked down and took a sip of water.

"How did you become a physics teacher?"

"What do you mean?"

"Well, uh . . . is physics something that you've always been passionate about?"

"I have to think about that. I'm not sure it's fair to say it was a passion, but I guess you could say that I had an interest. Compared to other subjects, at least."

"I see."

"How did you find physics?" he asked.

"Huh?"

"When you were in school."

"I know I learned the basics . . . not that I can remember any of that now. I was never good at physics, or any of the sciences, really. Anything that involved experiments or formulas was hard for me. I guess the books I've read aren't the only things I've forgotten."

This last remark made Mitsutsuka smile again, and I had to smile too. But then I was hit with an emotion that I had a hard time placing, a strange mixture of embarrassment and misery, and felt my face turn red once more. Looking down, I nodded several times.

After that, we fell into another period of silence, both of us gazing out the window. I glanced at the coffee cup by Mitsutsuka's hand and saw that it was practically empty. There was almost nothing left in my cup either. The clear glass sitting beside it was still half-full of water, and a small black bug had flown over and landed on the rim, like it was being pulled inside, only to flutter up into the air again and disappear. There were no other customers in the cafe, no sign of the lady who had served us. Mitsutsuka took care of the bill.

After leaving the cafe, we walked together to the station.

I saw a small park that I had failed to notice on the way, where an empty wire-mesh trash can lay on its side under a fuzzy yellow electric light, like something from a painting.

The night, as usual, was dotted here and there with different lights, which I watched without exactly seeing them, letting each foot fall in front of the other.

I thought about the walk I took that winter on my birthday.

I remembered that night, how I counted the lights, walking through coldness so profound that I could almost hear it, through that dry air slickened with so many special things. Before long, the hottest part of summer would be here, which would then give way to fall, followed by winter. And then that night would come again. As I took in the night, I looked over and saw that Mitsutsuka's shirt was glowing white, from his shoulders down his back.

It glowed in a way that reminded me of the smells of winter.

Floating in the tide of summer washing over us were signs and streetlights, lights from cars and countless other lights, but the light coming from Mitsutsuka's shirt was foreign to the summer night. I slowed down, walking a step behind so I could see his back. He slouched a little when he walked, and the shoulder carrying his mysteriously heavy brown nylon bag was thrust forward, forming a composition that for some reasons I associated with one word: teacher. Seen from behind, his back gave off a faint white glow, a sight that felt to me like a giant postcard, delivered to this moment from the winter.

When we got to the station, we purchased our tickets and bowed repeatedly to one another. Once we had each done this for a fair amount of time, we naturally stopped, and the two of us went through the gates, with neither in the lead. Since we were heading home in opposite directions, we parted at the passage that split off toward the staircases. On the way to the stairs, something made me turn around. At the other end,

Mitsutsuka was about to turn the corner. The next moment, in spite of myself, I yelled "Hey." As my voice shot through the air, an even louder sound rang through my heart, radiating through my body. My voice bounced off the low ceiling of the passageway and Mitsutsuka turned around. He gave me a quizzical look, then walked back over to me, leaning forward as he came. I walked toward him too. When we were close enough, I said his name again, then took two deep breaths. I said there was something that I'd forgotten to ask him about physics. "Sure," he said, looking at me. I looked back at him as I let out another sigh.

"It's about light. I don't know how much this has to do with physics, but I love looking at, um, light . . ." I can't pretend to understand why I was saying this to Mitsutsuka, or what I was hoping to achieve, but I let the words come out the way they wanted to.

"Light?" Mitsutsuka asked me.

I nodded over and over in response.

"By light, you mean light in general?" he asked.

I nodded over and over.

"It's just, I don't know . . . I guess it's nothing, but I really felt like, I forgot to tell you that, and felt like I had to tell you that today, before I lost the chance."

"Okay."

"Sorry to call your name like that," I said and bowed. "That was it. Sorry. That was everything I had to say. Sorry," I said, bowing as I backed away.

"No, I feel the same," Mitsutsuka said in a clear voice. I looked up at him.

"I like light, too," he said. "That's pretty much what got me into physics."

"Really?" I was stunned now, staring him in the face. "Really?"

"Really," Mitsutsuka said. "Light's a mystery. No one knows

what it is. Sometimes I think I've got it figured out, but I really don't. When I was a kid, I thought it was the strangest thing. I was so curious that I started studying it."

I stared at Mitsutsuka's face.

". . . I still think about light sometimes, even now."

"You do?"

"Sure."

"Um, do you think the light you're thinking about and the light I'm talking about are, um, the same thing?"

"Of course they are," Mitsutsuka said with a smile. "We're talking about the same light."

Upstairs on the platform, a voice announced that the train was now approaching. Mitsutsuka lifted his shoulder to adjust his bag, then turned to look at the stairs before looking me in the eye again.

"Well, next time, let's talk about light," Mitsutsuka said, then bowed slightly before walking off at a brisk pace. I watched him from behind, his left shoulder hanging low as he went. As he reached the end of the passageway and turned around the corner to the stairs, he looked back at me one more time, bowed, and disappeared.

For a while I just stood there, not moving, staring at the space that he'd left behind. I tried remembering all the things that I had seen and heard in the hour we had spent together—the coffee cups, Mitsutsuka's shoulders, the words we shared—but it was no use. Whenever I chased after a detail, I felt a motion in my chest. The feeling traveled into my palms and up my throat, making the dull pain flare.

5

I'm always going to the library to look things up, but I hardly ever go to bookstores anymore, unless I absolutely have to.

One time, I stopped by a bookstore and saw a stack of one of the novels I'd proofread. It was a joy to see the cover they'd chosen, but when I opened the book, I found an error staring back at me. Since then, I've found it hard to go anywhere near a book that is still fresh in my memory.

I was shocked to find a glaring error like that, jumping out at me, right there where anyone who cared to look would find it, despite my having checked every single line multiple times. But no matter how I looked at it, there it was, clear as day. I remember how it felt to walk home feeling that way, so depressed that I could hardly think straight. After I'd quit my old job and gone freelance, it had taken me a long time to develop my own way of doing things—and while I'm not saying I accomplished this, or that I attained anything close to confidence—this discovery left me feeling bewildered, as if whatever strength I'd managed to build up had been smashed to pieces.

When I found an error, it was my responsibility to correct it for the next printing. This meant I had to let whoever was in charge of the title know. In my case, this was Hijiri.

"Yeah, that's rough," she said, consoling me. "I know there's no such thing as a perfect book, but nothing breaks a proofreader's heart like a mistake you find after the book comes out."

Exactly, I thought, nodding deeply as I gripped the receiver, imagining Hijiri's face as she gripped the receiver just as hard and shook her head with all her heart.

Vowing to avoid any display of new releases, I entered a large bookstore for the first time in a while. It was overrun with people.

Women crowded the magazine racks near the entrance, practically piling on top of each other as they flipped through the pages. Keeping my distance, I went down a different aisle, heading for the back, and wandered for a while until I found the sign for the natural sciences section, where I started examining the spines.

The shelves were divided into different categories: math, physics, chemistry, cosmology, astronomy, engineering. Most of the books were massive and appeared to be specialized texts. I saw no signs that these books had been handled frequently. While there were a few eye-catching titles—*Fermat Ruined My Life* or *String Theory for the Scientifically Challenged*—I didn't know where to begin.

In the display area by my knees, I found stacks of books that looked like they were targeted at general readers, with illustrations or anime characters on every cover: *Hello, Goodbye: A New Theory of Relativity*, *The Physics of Finding Happiness*, *You + Math = Sexy*, and *Love and the Uncertainty Principle—A Guide to Romance*. I glanced at a few of them, but it was hard to know where to look or what to look for. I put them back where I found them, then scanned the shelves again, this time telling myself I'd look more carefully at the next book that had the word "light" in the title.

For a whole week, I couldn't stop thinking about what Mitsutsuka told me just before we said goodbye. *Next time, we can talk about light.* Maybe he was just being polite, but if the day really did come when he and I could talk about light, I thought I'd better know something, so I came to the bookstore to see what I could find.

Unable to find a book I liked, I left the lonely shelves of technical material. Customers stalled by the entrance or stood in line by the registers, holding books. I turned down another aisle to avoid the crowds.

I approached a bright set of shelves, where the spines were almost uniformly pink. A group of girls was looking through the books and chatting away. Judging from the titles I could see, this was where they kept the self-help books for women, with keywords like marriage, choices, romance, dreams, and destiny written in dazzling fonts, leaping from their colorful covers.

All the girls had dyed their hair the same shade of brown and wore it in the same style. Their makeup was even the same, like they were on some kind of team. Their tops revealed so much cleavage that I was worried that their breasts would spill out as soon as they bent over, but they didn't seem the least bit concerned, so I felt sort of ashamed for having thought of such a thing. Their legs, where not covered by their miniskirts, were visibly bruised. They wore high heels, laughing in loud voices as they showed each other things that they'd found in the books they were reading. I had an eye on them as I stopped a fair distance away and picked up a full-color book called *The One Thing You Need to Do By Thirty-Five*. Looking at the table of contents, I could see that the book offered not one but a complete list of things to do by thirty-five, divided into sections such as work, marriage, and motherhood, each with subtopics like savings, insurance, engagement presents, wedding ceremonies, married life, and pregnancy, and replete with precious illustrations. I slipped a finger into the middle of the book and turned to a random page, where I found the large words "The Importance of Partnership," under which the main text, laid out a font almost as big began by stating that it's perfectly normal for a woman to be worried that she'll have to give up a lot to get married and start a family, but that these experiences offer plenty in return, so talk things over with a trusted partner and embrace the joys of womanhood to the fullest. I gave the rest a quick look before putting it back and picking up the book next to it, *Be an Amazon—What's Wrong with Being Strong?* This book passionately advocated for women to live independent lives, supplementing the argument with a variety of tables giving statistics and a sampling of detailed simulations that projected what a woman could expect to save by different ages over her lifetime (although the average salaries and savings listed in these tables were so far from my own that I was sure there must have been some mistake). I skipped around, reading a line or two from more or less every page before moving on to something else. This one was called *Thus Spoke the Queen of Hearts*, with a cover featuring a model who looked like a mannequin. Her nipples and crotch were barely hidden behind a silky cloth. This one, too, was laid out using giant print that brought to mind an eye exam, with an occasional close-up photo of the lines on a moist pair of women's lips or an archetypal butt. This book argued that being loved is what makes a woman beautiful, meaning the more romance the better, and that romance is a resource that no one can put a price on, and sex provides a woman with more than just pleasure, significantly influencing the unavoidable experience of menopause for those who have enjoyed a fulfilling sex life in their younger years. After I read a little more, I picked up a different book, which I took a quick look at before reaching for another. At some point, I felt as though I was being watched and looked up to find a girl looking back at me. She was part of a different group from earlier, but essentially the same kind of girl. When she saw me looking back, she turned away and went back to talking with the others.

I flipped through half a dozen or so more books. *Stocks to Turn Your Luck Around*, *Makeup Magic: Increase Your Salary Seventeen-Fold*, *Bad Women Are Better at Everything*, and *The Beauty, the Saint, the Madonna—How I Became a Legend*, in which a seasoned actress I'd never heard of, but who was evidently pretty famous, offers an unflinching confessional account of her sexual adventures. I don't know how long I had been standing there, but eventually I realized that my big toe had fallen asleep, probably because my sneakers were a little tight.

Heading for the main exit of the bookstore as I made my way through the growing throng of customers, I made it outside and walked back to the station without ever looking up. Whenever I passed people, I was left with bits of laughter or a fun conversation ringing in my ears.

As I passed below the haloes of the green and red traffic signals, I was taken by this strange view of the evening, the city streets full of people—people waiting, the people they were waiting for, people out to eat together, people going somewhere together, people heading home together. I allowed my thoughts to settle on the brightness filling their hearts and lungs, squinting as I walked along and counted all the players of this game that I would never play.

I passed through the ticket gate and got on the train, which rumbled down the tracks to my station, where I went up the stairs and back onto the street, by which time the sensation had returned to my toe, albeit with a subtle itchiness. As I walked home with my mind wandering, I thought about the books that I had looked through in the bookstore. It occurred to me that they were full of things that people wanted to say to other people, or things people wanted somebody to say to them. Should you choose romance or work? Was it possible to have both? Should you choose to live your life alone, or should you choose to share your life with someone else? Should you have kids or not? What were the pros and cons? What did each choice force you to give up? What did you stand to gain?

There are people who spend every day immersed in these considerations—like the younger women I saw standing by the shelves—following the trajectories detailed in these books, doing things to become happier, to become better versions of themselves. These women had so many choices, and so many temptations, so many layers of coincidences and incidents, and the choices they made would change the color of their lives. They were surrounded by possibility.

As I recalled the various things the books had to say, ruminating over their choice of language, they almost seemed to harmonize into a secret message that would lead me somewhere, anywhere but here. I stood alone before a thick gate made from stacks of colorful book covers, no way of knowing what was on the other side, or where it led, or what exactly I could expect to find there, and of course there was no one there to guide me. All I knew for certain was that this place had nothing to do with me.

One week later, I got an email from Mitsutsuka. It was the last Sunday of July.

* * *

"This summer's a hot one, huh?"

Mitsutsuka was wearing the same outfit, sitting in the same seat at the same cafe, where we had met two weeks before.

The air conditioning was on so high that for a moment you would swear your skin was tightening up. I put away the handkerchief that I was using to dab sweat from my forehead and waited for the remaining sweat to evaporate. It took a second to catch up and return to what Mitsutsuka had asked me, but

I replied and said it really had been hot, then nodded a few times at my own words. The woman from last time was nowhere to be found. In her place, a white-haired man with a buzz cut and a full black beard came over to take our orders: a coffee for Mitsutsuka and the same for me.

"Was it this hot last summer?"

"Last summer . . ." I said, thinking it over, but I couldn't remember, so I stopped talking. It was almost to the point where I was unsure whether there had even been a summer last year. But that could have been because of all the sake I had on my way out of the house.

"Are you on summer vacation now?" I asked.

"I am. Until September."

"And you can do whatever you want over the break?"

"I suppose so," Mitsutsuka said, looking a bit unsure.

Same as the time before, we were the only two customers. Through the silence, I could just hear the music playing, a piano repeating a melody I felt like I'd heard before, though of course I had no idea whose song it was.

Outside the window, nearly everything in view was radiant with summer light, and if you squinted it would almost look as if a special powder had been sprinkled all around.

I couldn't maintain eye contact with Mitsutsuka, so I blinked over and over and diverted my attention to the light of summer. With every blink, I felt my feelings occupy more space, only to mellow as they grew. I was disoriented by an awareness of living through the very scene that I had been envisioning for nights on end before falling asleep. My heartbeat drummed beneath my ears.

"Are you going anywhere this summer?" Mitsutsuka suddenly asked.

"I'm not going anywhere," I responded, in a voice so loud that, when I heard myself, I blushed and tried again, this time quietly. "Not really, I guess."

"No?" Mitsutsuka asked and took a sip of water.

"What about you?" I asked. "Any plans?"

"No, I'm not going anywhere, either." Mitsutsuka smiled as if he didn't know what to say.

"Is that normal for you?"

"In the summer?" he asked.

"Uh-huh."

"I think so. I never go anywhere."

"You don't have to go to school during the break?"

"I used to go to school during the summer, back when I was a club advisor, but since stepping down I've had an actual summer break, same as the students."

"What was the club?" I asked, after swallowing my spit to stifle a rising hiccup. The pungent smell of sake filled my mouth.

"Classical Appreciation."

"As in classical music?"

"That's right," Mitsutsuka said.

"You mean the club meets up at school over vacation, to listen to music?"

"Not every day, but yes," he said. "They go to concerts a few times a year, and the school has a good audio set-up, which the club gets to use. The kids read music criticism, too, and try writing some of their own."

"So you like classical music?" I asked.

"Well, I didn't listen to it before. I was actually pretty old by the time I started. But I remember one time, when I was a kid, being amazed by a Horowitz piece a friend played for me. It wasn't enough to hook me at the time, but when I finally listened to a few other things, I realized it was actually pretty great, and even went around listening to things here and there for a while."

"So you must know a lot . . ." I asked as I let out a cough.

"Far from it," Mitsutsuka laughed. "I don't know anything

at all. The things we listened to in the club were just as new to me as they were to the students."

"Really?"

"After about three years with the club, we got a new teacher who really knew his stuff, and I let him take over."

The bearded man who took our orders brought the coffee. Our cups were rattling on a silver tray, which he then set down on the table between us. We stared at the drinks and waited for him to leave before we tried them.

"Do you have a favorite instrument?" I asked, then instantly regretted it, as I didn't know the first thing about musical instruments.

"I like the piano."

Predictably, I was unable to think of a single pianist.

"What about you?" Mitsutsuka asked. "Do you like music?"

"I don't really listen to music. I never have."

"I see."

As this had thrown a wrench in our conversation, I squeezed the handle of my cup with enough force to turn my thumbnail white and brought the coffee to my lips, glanced down for a moment, then took another sip. Fending off a sigh, I glanced out the window, where a group of elementary school kids wearing yellow hats and carrying backpacks were crossing the street at the traffic light, messing around and having fun.

"When I was a kid, it always felt like summer vacation lasted forever," I said, letting the words come out before I thought them over. I hiccupped, but I decided I wasn't going to worry about that. I could hear my own voice, yet it didn't sound like I was doing the talking. The kids reached the other side of the white-hot crosswalk and disappeared up the street.

"Well, some people say it feels that way for kids because they haven't been around for long, or had that much experience with time," Mitsutsuka said. "Of course, there's no way to prove that."

"Does that mean that the longer we live, the more it feels like time speeds up?" I asked.

"I suppose so. That's the idea, at least."

"Is that a part of physics?"

"Maybe," Mitsutsuka laughed. "It's definitely related, but I think time has more to do with math. Do you mind if I ask you something?"

"Sure."

"What were you like as a kid?"

"As a kid?" I tried to read Mitsutsuka's expression. "Normal, I guess?"

"Did you play outside a lot?"

I shook my head.

". . . Um, I was usually inside. Always, actually. Not because I was a good student, or because I liked to read or anything. I honestly have no idea what I was doing, but I know that I was almost always home."

"Really?"

"Yeah, and I didn't even like it there."

I took a sip of my coffee. It had gotten a little cold.

"I guess I spent a lot of time sleeping. I really spent a lot of time asleep, probably half the day, like it was nothing. When I woke up, my head would hurt from oversleeping. So I'd just go back to sleep."

This made Mitsutsuka laugh.

"Even if I wasn't sleeping . . . I liked to sit there, doing nothing. I would close my eyes like this. But I wasn't thinking about anything, either. Nothing at all."

When I closed my eyes and breathed in through my nose, my head began to sway. I smelled the smells of drying grass. Looking out upon the bright white light of summer in the yard, I went into my room, and in no time, the whole world was blanketed in soft shadows, my little body, still the body of a child, lying motionless in the blue dark. The next thing I knew, the cicadas that had been buzzing all around me were scared away, and the weave of the tatami melted under my fingertips. I reached to catch it, but the outline of my body started to fade and an image I could never forget flashed through my heart. I opened my eyes and looked at Mitsutsuka.

". . . Actually, I just remembered something," I said. "I spent a lot of time back then as a lion."

"A lion?" Mitsutsuka looked back at me, raising his droopy eyebrows. His eyes went round so quickly that I laughed.

"Your eyes just got so round."

"Did they? Well, eyeballs are round to begin with, so it's not actually my eyes. Just the position of my eyelids."

"Right." Now I was grinning. "But they got round all of a sudden, like this."

"Did they?" Mitsutsuka asked, sounding a little bashful. He drank some water, then asked, "So . . . when you say you spent time as a lion, does that mean roaring like a lion?" He started wiping his hands clean with his oshibori as he spoke.

"No, I never roared," I laughed. "This happened when I was sleeping. I mean, I slept like a normal person, or maybe not exactly normal. Because the whole time I was sleeping, I could see a lion."

"A lion," Mitsutsuka nodded.

"Yeah. A lioness. Bare skin, no fur," I said. "She's in the middle of a savanna. Nothing but grass as far as the eye can see. Every now and then, the wind blows and cuts across the grass like a green wave. It's so peaceful. And there's the lioness. It's not long after her hunt, so her stomach's full, and there's nothing for her to do. Nothing at all. She has no fear, no worries, no homework or any other work—those are just human ideas that mean nothing to her . . . Her body's strong and so's her heart, so no one dares to bother her . . . She runs through the grass, eats her fill, then curls up under the shade of a tree. That's where she sleeps until her eyes open again. The breeze feels nice and the grass smells like home. Everything is quiet, humming with energy, her paws are full of power. Thinking about nothing, sleeping the whole day . . . When she sleeps, the lion's entire world is sleep. So she sleeps . . . She gives herself to sleep . . . And nothing else exists, not a single thought, only sleep. It's as if when she's asleep, sleep and the world are one and the same." I spun my neck around and blinked slowly. "That was how I slept when I was little."

Mitsutsuka made a face like he was thinking. Then, as if it had suddenly occurred to him, he asked if I still slept this way.

I said of course not and laughed. It was a deranged, staccato laugh that came out of my nose, and even seemed to free some mucus, which I hurriedly wiped away with a finger, but real- ized I was thankfully mistaken. The alcohol was really having an effect on me, much more than when I first arrived, and it felt like the more I talked the deeper it would seep into my body. My head and my eyelids were heavy, but I felt light and relaxed, and most of all, it allowed me to step away from myself and genuinely enjoy a sense of distance from my usual anxieties.

"I'm no lion these days. I can't believe I'd forgotten about that until now. It's like it never even happened. I bet if we weren't having this conversation I never would have remem- bered," I said as I nodded slowly.

"Maybe not," Mitsutsuka said, nodding with me. Then he suggested, calling me Ms. Irie again, that I might hold off on the coffee and have some water instead.

I grinned. "No, no, I'm fine with this," I said, then gave him another big grin.

"Memory's funny, isn't it? We remember some things out of nowhere, but so much of what happens, we never think about again."

"That's true."

"And if that's true, what's memory anyway?" I shook my

head and crossed my arms. "I mean, there are way too many things you'll never remember. Sometimes a memory jumps out at you, even though almost everything is lost forever. But what if all the things that we can't remember are actually the most important ones?" At this point, something inside me cracked, and I began to laugh out loud.

Once I started laughing, it was hard to make myself stop, so I just laughed some more.

Mitsutsuka waited for me to finish laughing, then smiled.

"It's strange," he said.

"It is," I said, smiling back at him.

Leaving the cafe, we walked together to the station, side by side, the same as last time.

The asphalt gleamed, its overwhelming whiteness somehow leaving me disoriented and I was scared that I might trip. I had packed a new thermos of sake in my bag, so I could have some when I started feeling sober, but it seemed like there wouldn't be any need. If anything, I felt in sync with the entire world, like my chest was opening to the horizon, and everything before me was a part of me, flowing in and out of me, coolly and freely.

Reaching out my hands, my fingertips could easily have stretched into infinity. As feathery as I felt overall, my footsteps landed squarely on the boundlessly white asphalt. Feeling that way, I walked beside Mitsutsuka. The sky was blue, but between the buildings in the distance and the telephone poles in front of us, I saw a thunderhead so perfectly fluffy that it looked fake—like it had just been created out of nothing. I stopped and pointed up at it.

"That thing is crazy! Crazy . . . huge!"

Mitsutsuka covered his eyes with his hand and looked up at the cloud for a moment, jutting out his chin.

"Look at that blue color," I said.

"Blue collar?"

"Blue color. Of the sky," I said, clearly pronouncing every syllable.

"Right, the color blue. Absolutely," Mitsutsuka said, speaking quickly and nodding in agreement.

For a while we just stood there, gazing at the towering mass of cloud. If the shapely contours of the cloud made it look fake, the blueness of the sky around it was so perfect that it almost made me uneasy. There was no variation, no depth, as if a dome of the most absolute blue possible had been placed quietly above us.

"Why is the sky blue?" I asked Mitsutsuka after a little while. "I mean, why does it look so blue?"

"It has to do with wavelengths," he said, gazing at the cloud while his hand shielded his eyes, the same as before. "The shorter the wavelength, the more it scatters. Blue is really short, which is why the sky looks so vast and far away."

"Hmm," I looked at Mitsutsuka's face, the half that I could see. "I don't get it."

"Don't get it, huh?" Mitsutsuka looked at me and laughed out loud. "I hear that a lot."

He scratched the skin along his nose.

"Basically, the light of the sun isn't a single color. It's made up of an infinite range of colors."

"Infinite?"

"Right. Well, let's just say it's all these different colors, blending together. So, if you're out in space, where there's nothing, there's nothing to catch the light. A ray of light could shoot right past you, but the human eye wouldn't be able to see it. We can only see light when it reflects off something."

"We can't see light on its own?"

"That's right," Mitsutsuka said. "When we see something, the reason we can see it is because it's being hit with light. Even parts of the sky where it looks like there's nothing there, like the atmosphere, contain molecules, so I guess the simplest way to put it is, what reflects off of those molecules is what we see."

"Okay," I said.

"But color's also got to do with wavelengths. The shorter ones look blue to us, and the longer ones look red. Out of all the light that comes down from the sun, the blue parts scatter the most. That's why the blue spreads further and further away, until the sky looks enormous, like it does right now."

Steadying my foggy head with my hand, I looked up at the sky in silence. For a moment, Mitsutsuka did the same.

". . . In the evening, the blue light scatters even more, leaving the red to take over. That's how we get the skies we see at sunset."

"So when light scatters, it's kind of like how paint thins when you spread it?"

"Well, not exactly, but in a way."

I hummed vaguely and glanced at Mitsutsuka's face again. He had single eyelids, and at the corner of one eye, there was a small but conspicuous scar. The hair over his ears was sticking out a little, and I could see traces of sweat around his temples.

"Here's an example of color and reflection," Mitsutsuka said, pointing at a tree I couldn't name, planted along the sidewalk. "See those leaves? We can see them because the light is hitting them, right? But the reason they look green to us, simplifying things a bit, is because of how they're absorbing all the different colors of light coming from the sun, except for green, which they reflect. Of course, to be precise, it isn't only one color reflecting off the leaves, but, well, our eyes see what's left as the color green."

"So the leaves soak up the light?" I asked. "They suck it up?"

"They do. And it's not just leaves. It's different for things that emit their own light, like TVs or computer screens, but when we see something that has color, the color that we see is the color that hasn't been absorbed."

"Uh-huh," I said, nodding.

Mitsutsuka looked me square in the face.

"So, putting it simply," I said, "the color that we're seeing is whatever's left behind."

"Exactly."

"Sounds like books," I said as the thought occurred to me.

"Like books?" Mitsutsuka asked.

". . . As in, there's no perfect book, with no mistakes," I said. "There's always a mistake hiding somewhere."

"Always?"

"Always," I laughed. "Books are so full of mistakes, it almost makes me wonder if they only exist so that the mistakes can pass their genes on to another generation."

"No kidding," he said.

"Of course, there comes a point when you have to stop looking. You have to let go, but the mistakes are still there, always."

"When do you find that out?"

"Sooner or later."

"So the mistakes aren't there, until you find them . . ."

"Right," I said, nodding slowly.

"I don't know, constantly looking for mistakes like that . . ." Mitsutsuka sounded pensive. "Doesn't that wear you down a little? To keep looking for something you've decided is definitely there, when you can't really say for sure?"

"That's a good question." I smiled, tilting my head to the side. "Does it wear me down . . . Maybe? I don't know, it's hard to say. Did I make it sound that way?"

"No," he said. "I suppose it's typical enough to devote yourself to looking for something that may or may not actually be there, all the while telling yourself it has to be . . . I guess I was thinking . . . if what you're looking for isn't some essential truth or correct answer, but mistakes or errors, that has to be hard . . . That's really interesting to me."

"You mean it sounds kind of hopeless?" I laughed.

Mitsutsuka said that wasn't what he meant.

"Who knows." I shook my head. "I've been doing this and only this for so long now, I don't even know what it feels like to do something else."

A silence ensued, but the fast-approaching sound of bells broke through as several bicycles shot between us on the sidewalk. Jumping out of the way, I stumbled and lost my bearings, almost landing in some plants. Mitsutsuka asked me if I was okay. I bowed and said that I was fine.

"You were just asking if it sounds hopeless," Mitsutsuka said a moment later. "But if your goal is to make a book, in that sense, you have to have something—hope or something pretty close to it."

I looked at Mitsutsuka. My eyes stung, like I was going to cry. Somewhere a bird let out a small chirp. It was a call I'd never heard before.

As if this had been some kind of a cue, the two of us suddenly went silent. Then, a moment later, we just started walking. I lagged a little, walking behind him, but slightly off to the side, so that I could get a good look at his back, same as last time, as I put one foot in front of the other. I watched the worn heels of his sneakers, the places where his bag was fraying, noting the way he walked, the shape of his shoulders, and the length of his neck, but before I knew it, we'd made it to the station.

Without saying anything, we purchased our tickets, went through the ticket gates, and walked toward the stairs, but just before we headed off in opposite directions, Mitsutsuka pulled a book out of his bag as if it just occurred to him, and offered it to me.

"I almost forgot. I have to give you this, otherwise meeting up today would have been for nothing." Holding the book in one hand, Mitsutsuka adjusted the strap of his bag. "This is the one I emailed you about. It's a good book. I know you said you like light, so . . ."

I took the book in my hands. It was on the thicker side and wrapped in a clear plastic bag. After examining the cover, I made a special place for it inside my bag and thanked him for letting me borrow it.

"No, please keep it. I have another copy."

Mitsutsuka gestured graciously, then raised his hand as a goodbye. "See you," he said as he turned around and walked off, heading straight for the stairs, the same as the last time. I stared into his back as he went, paying close attention to the way he looked from behind—how the cuffs of his beige slacks were turned up, revealing his white socks, how his left shoulder sagged a little, so it looked like he was leaning to one side, how his tucked-in polo made a weird bulge just under the waistband of his slacks. As he was about to go up the stairs, Mitsutsuka looked my way and nodded slightly, but rounded the corner before I could nod back.

For a while after he was gone, I just stood there, same as last time, eyes on the dirty white wall at the base of the stairs. Pretty soon I heard a voice on the tracks announcing the arrival of a train, followed by the frenetic beeping that signaled its departure and the sound of footsteps coming down the stairs. Even after Mitsutsuka's train had left the station, I stood there in the same place, staring blankly at the wall, which failed to show me anything at all, no matter how long I kept my eyes on it.

* * *

The Monday after Obon, I got a call from Hijiri.

"That was the first real vacation I've taken in years!"

Hijiri laughed and asked me in a sunny voice how I was feeling.

"I'm doing well," I said.

"I'm glad I could take a break for once, but Obon's crazy. Everywhere you go, it's expensive and crowded. Way worse than I expected. I'm not doing that again next year."

Hijiri had spent five nights and six days on Ko Samui.

"That's Thailand, right?"

"Yeah. You have to take another plane once you get to Bangkok. I thought it was going to be close, but it was actually pretty far."

"Wow."

"I don't know, I guess it's a nice place to hang out and do nothing." I heard Hijiri let out a tiny yawn.

I felt like asking whether she had gone alone, but something held me back. Instead, I let Hijiri tell me all about the elephant she rode, and the beauty treatment that she got on Ko Samui.

"Before the break, I was actually working on a book set in Thailand. A novel. The book was full of pretty dark stuff, and a lot of it had to do with elephants. I'm not really the type to care about that kind of thing, not that I'm the type to fly to Thailand to ride an elephant, either. Believe me, it wasn't my idea, but the guy I was with said he wanted to, so we did it. And it was insane. The trainer kept jabbing the elephant's ear with a sharp poker to control it. He told it where to go, and how fast to go. I know elephants have tough skin, so I'm not sure how much it bothers them, but they definitely bleed. It's not like the elephants can tell us how they feel, or even benefit directly from the money stupid tourists like us are shelling out, but the second I got on the thing, sure enough, I felt completely disgusted."

"Like it was too much?"

"Kinda," Hijiri said, then sighed. "I mean, I know that I'm in no position to say anything, not after we spent what over there is pretty much a small fortune to ride around on some elephant for literally no good reason."

"So, why did the guy you went with want to ride an elephant?"

"Beats me. He probably thought it'd be fun. Maybe he figured it'd be a way to, I dunno, commemorate the occasion. That's got to be it. He's the type who always sees the sunny side of things. Wait, hold on, I'm not trying to say that I'm this incredibly sensitive soul, forever lost in deep thoughts. But there are these people in the world who are, like, optimistic by default. They never think about anything dark. I have no idea where that kind of unbridled positivity even comes from, but I guess some people are born that way. That's what this guy is like. I mean, I guess it's probably better to be like that than to get hung up about every little thing."

I took a breath. "So have you two been together for a while?" I asked.

"Huh?" Hijiri sounded shocked, then laughed. "We aren't together. It isn't like that."

"Okay," I said. Then I was quiet. Hijiri yawned again and told me how she could never get enough sleep these days, no matter how much she slept, despite having been free of jet lag for a while now. After a sigh, she started telling me about the unbelievably large shrimp she ate where she was staying, how cheap it was and how they'd prepared it.

"How come you won't date him, though?"

I asked this really casually, as if I didn't care, slipping it in at the perfect time.

"Who? That guy?" Hijiri was incredulous. "I mean, I don't know. I don't feel that way about him."

"Really?"

"Yeah."

"So, how do you feel about him?" Holding my cell phone right up to my ear, I walked into the kitchen, opened the fridge, took out a beer, and drank about half the can right where I stood.

"How do I feel about him . . . I mean, I like him, but I don't *like* like him," Hijiri said. "At this age, I honestly don't see any relationships starting from those kinds of feelings, or from two people saying that they like each other. Almost everybody gets involved before they ever talk about their feelings. I mean, that's really the only way. Why bother acting like we're teenagers, making all these big promises? Of course whether you're exclusive or not is a big deal, if you're thinking about marriage or whatever. But it's actually pretty fun not liking somebody too much."

"Fun in what way?"

"Plenty of ways," she said. "You can be more generous."

"Generous?"

"I know, who am I, right? What I mean is, you don't get caught up in all the annoying stuff. When it's just for fun, it's pretty rare that anyone gets hurt. You can focus on sharing the good times with each other."

"But you're not officially dating, right?"

"Hey, what's up with you today?" Hijiri sounded incredibly pleased. "I don't think I've ever heard you like this. Did something happen?"

I squeezed the can and found that it still had beer inside. I told her nothing was going on, then sat down on the sofa before switching the phone to my left hand.

"Anyway," Hijiri said, "for me, I don't really know what it means to be with someone anymore. Besides, even if you feel that way about somebody, whether or not you can really connect is a whole different thing."

"Connect?"

Hijiri snorted.

"It's fine to like somebody, but that doesn't mean they'll feel the same way, and it's not necessarily a good thing if they do. I'm not saying it's good to settle or anything, but maybe there's actually nothing wrong with kinda liking someone, being kinda involved."

Thinking over what Hijiri had said, I stood up for no reason, then sat back down on the sofa.

"I don't know if thirty-four years is a long time or not," Hijiri said, "but if there's anything I've learned in life this far, it's not to take things seriously across the board."

"Across the board?"

"That's right. As long as you're living on this planet, you have to be serious about something, but it's better to be serious about a limited number of things."

Hijiri laughed a little and added that she knew this was old news, and people had been saying it forever, but that she thought there was some truth in it.

"Personally," she said, "I've got a lot of things I'd rather focus on than romance. And hey, I'm sure this sounds like a pretty asinine thing to say, but what's it mean to like somebody anyway?"

I answered vaguely again, put the empty beer can on the floor, and nodded.

"For me," she said, "it's not just about liking. I've never really understood any of my own emotions."

"Your own emotions?"

"Yeah. I wonder how long it's been this way. I can't remember, not that I'm trying to . . . but when it comes to emotions, feelings, moods, all those things, I can never figure out where mine end and other people's begin."

I picked up the empty can and brought it to my lips, biting gently on the rim as I listened to Hijiri speak.

"I don't know, I guess sometimes I feel happy or sad or worried . . . or maybe I get really into something on TV, or really like the flavor of some giant shrimp, whatever. But sometimes I have to wonder if those thoughts or feelings might be coming from the things I read for work. When I start to feel emotional about something, I can't tell if I'm actually feeling that way. What if it's just something somebody wrote in a book? Or maybe a line or a performance from some movie . . . Either way, I get this feeling like I'm quoting somebody else's work."

"Quoting?"

"Yeah, like the feelings aren't mine."

"You mean they don't feel real?"

"Not exactly. It's different. It feels completely real. That's what makes it so stupid," she said. "It feels real on every level. It kinda messes with my head. But I can't accept it, not entirely. So like, whenever I start thinking something, or feeling something, these stupid questions start going through my head. Whenever my emotions or whatever kick in, my world goes blank—like something's taken over me. Then I start doubting everything, like, what if my whole life was just a quote from something else, only I never realized it? That's where my brain goes."

I nodded.

"I mean, that feeling like none of this is mine, like it's just something I picked up somewhere, sometimes I start to think that maybe even that's something I ripped off. I'm a real lost cause, I know." At that point, Hijiri laughed out loud. "When it comes to love, the only weapon that we've got is our emotions, right? So what can you do when your foundation's all messed up? If that's the state you're in, there's no way you can ever get serious with anybody."

"You're serious about your work, though . . . right?" I asked.

"Sure," she said. "I mean, I know it can look like work's about interpersonal relationships, but it isn't about people at all. It's just a matter of structures. Situations. Sometimes work pisses me off, but I never let it leave a mark. I know I vent about that stuff a lot, but I'm like a brick wall. Nothing gets to me, ever. And trust me, the idea that I've ripped off the way I feel about my work has definitely crossed my mind, too. I must've picked that one up somewhere. I'm pretty sure I did.

I feel like that's exactly why work is the only place where I let myself be serious. There's no way you could approach everything in life with the same attitude, because that'd be total nonsense. For me, work is the only thing that I really have to do. And that stupid crap we talked about that other time, yeah, that kind of stuff makes me angry—stupidly angry—but that anger is, well, it's my own problem, and at the same time it's actually not. And that's why I'm fine with all my feelings being derivative, and why it's actually a problem if they're not, because I kinda need them to be. That way I can go on being pissed off, precisely because what I'm feeling is someone else's anger, someone else's rage, someone else's feelings."

"You mean, like . . . righteous indignation?" I opened the fridge. After thinking for a moment, I decided against another beer, instead reaching for the small bottle of sake that had caught my eye. I held the phone against my ear, twisted off the cap, and took a sip.

"Not at all," Hijiri laughed. "This little bubble of mine is a bit too sunny, too comfy for me to be anything close to indignant. I mean, after everything I've said, I guess it comes down to this. No matter whose emotions they are, I just don't like them. That's all."

Hijiri went on to explain how everything was nice and light with the guy who went on the trip with her, but she was finding new things to dislike about him all the time, and she'd probably break it off pretty soon. She had other people she could sleep with or go out to eat with, but she had started thinking that maybe these things weren't so important to her after all. She came back from vacation to find herself with a real mess on her hands: a difference of opinion between an author and a proofreader.

Listening to Hijiri talk about these things, I imagined what Mitsutsuka looked like from behind, pushing through the turnstiles and heading toward the stairs. Then, closing my eyes,

I tried envisioning his face. I remembered the wrinkles all over it, the deep creases at the corners of his eyes, the little scar. Then I thought about his voice, which was neither high nor low, not unusual in any way. When I thought about Mitsutsuka, these three things were the best that I could do, no matter how I probed my memory.

As Hijiri continued, a thought emerged in my mind. I knew almost nothing about Mitsutsuka. I didn't know his age, or his first name, or where he lived, or when I would see him again.

6

I had sex for the first time in my final year of high school. My school was geared toward mediocre students, kids who weren't exactly good or bad at studying. From an early age, I'd always had a hard time being in groups or socializing, which meant I didn't really have any enemies, but it also made it harder to make friends.

That year, I was put into a new class with Noriko Hayakawa.

Whenever I saw her on the train, she was alone, reading a book, wearing bright white socks that I could see under her heavy-looking skirt. I saw her all the time, but we never exchanged words, though I was curious about her and how the dark blue school bag at her feet had none of the flashy, jangly keychains favored by most of the other girls.

Once we were in the same class, we started talking a little when we saw each other on the train or at the station, and before long, without even discussing it, we were riding the train to school and back together. Noriko spoke in a quiet voice that shook in a puzzling way, like it was blowing in the wind, and said that because she had been teased about it ever since she was little, it made her self-conscious and resistant to talking.

"Voices are important," Noriko said with a little laugh.

"But, I don't know, it's not as bad as you think," I said.

"Sure . . . at least it's better now. When I was little, it was way worse . . . really bad, like I was breathing out the words instead of speaking. I sounded really weird."

"Do you ever sing?" I asked.

Noriko gave me an awkward smile.

"Singing is the last thing I'd ever do . . . I don't even know how. I wouldn't know where to start. I've never tried."

"Never?" I asked, a little shocked.

"Yeah . . . Not even for music class." As she spoke, Noriko tucked her hair behind her ear, away from her cheek. "I'm pretty sure my vocal cords are deformed."

As the train rocked side to side, I imagined Noriko's little vocal cords, inside her chest, under her white shirt collar, but I had no idea what vocal cords were actually supposed to look like or even where they were.

Noriko was an only child. Her family ran a large factory where they specialized in making sweaters. She said that sometimes she helped out, designing little animal patches that they added for decoration. She showed me several of the drawings she had done in her notebook. There were all kinds of creatures with funny ears, sketched out in thin mechanical pencil, and the pages were a smudgy gray, as if they'd been rubbed over and over with an eraser.

"It's usually old ladies who buy our sweaters," Noriko said. "Actually, they're the only ones. You know how big supermarkets have those sections with stacks and stacks of clothes? We make the sweaters you see in places like that."

"Really?"

"Yeah. They sell well, too. And the sweaters with some kind of accent sell a whole lot better than the plain ones. One tiny detail like that is enough to make the ladies feel like they're getting something special."

"Your designs are so amazing, though. I suck at drawing," I said, telling the truth. With that, Noriko looked down at the open pages of her notebook, sighed, then smiled a little.

"It's no big deal. Anything works. It could be a mouse, a

cat, a tiger. As long as it's nice and fluffy . . . No one even looks hard enough to see what kind of animal it is. Nobody cares."

"Really?"

"Yeah. So I just mix them all together and draw whatever I want. It could be a rabbit or a cat or a mouse or a tiger or a horse or a sheep . . . because it kind of looks like all of them combined."

"That actually sounds pretty hard to do," I said, glancing at the notebook. We spent some time staring at the faces of the animals she had drawn. Every one of them had the same little ribbon tied around its neck.

"Honestly, you have no idea how many sweaters we sell. How many sweaters do you have?" asked Noriko.

"Not that many. Maybe two?"

"Fair enough . . . Somehow our sweaters keep on selling, though. It's crazy. Every day, somebody's buying our sweaters. At this point, there can't be anyone who doesn't have one. I mean . . . every single week, I see these giant shipments leave the factory, like a whole mountain of sweaters, and it really makes me think. It's kind of mind-boggling. Piles and piles of sweaters, all shaped like upper bodies, with price tags on them . . . carried off somewhere, put on display. They're brought home and become part of someone's outfit, somebody I don't know the first thing about. I dunno, it's hard to wrap my head around it."

"Yeah," I nodded.

"But those sweaters are how my parents raised me," Noriko laughed. "My family's been able to get by thanks to the steady stream of people who go out and buy these cheap sweaters with goofy animals on them."

"I bet my mom's got one," I said and laughed.

"Next time you see her in a sweater, check and see if it's got an animal patch on it." Now Noriko was laughing too.

"I'm sure it's busy in the winter . . . but what do you sell in the summer?" The question had just occurred to me, but I went ahead and asked. Noriko looked at me like I was crazy.

"Summer sweaters. People love summer sweaters."

A little while later, Noriko gave me a dark blue sweater featuring a cat patch. "I have the same one," she said in a quiet, shaky voice and smiled. I debated what to get her in return, but wound up going with some nail clippers I found at a little shop in my neighborhood. Once it got cold, I wore the sweater over a shirt and sometimes even wore it to school. I wore that sweater for a long time after graduation, long after I stopped seeing Noriko. But even back when we were hanging out, it's not like we met up outside of school or went places together. The only time we spent together was before and after school. We never talked about anything that mattered, but Noriko was the first person I could call a friend. That's what she meant to me.

One day after school, I was rushing out of my last class to catch Noriko down at the gate when I almost ran headfirst into Mizuno. He was in my class, and we'd been in calligraphy club together, but we'd barely ever spoken, at least that I could remember.

Sorry, I said, rushing an apology. I was about to walk away when I heard Mizuno say something back. I wasn't sure what he said, so I just stood there until he said it again. "Did you quit?" Since we'd never really spoken before, I didn't know what he was talking about, or how to respond, so I just stood there by the door, saying nothing.

"The club," he said, looking at me.

Toward the beginning of senior year, after two years of lukewarm membership, I stopped going to calligraphy club. There was no special reason. I just stopped. Lots of students had come and gone while I was there, and the advisor and the other members never really seemed to care. I never thought that anyone had missed me being around, so when I realized Mizuno was talking about that club, I was confused.

I nodded and said "Yeah," then he said "Okay," and went into the classroom.

Mizuno was always so quiet. He barely spoke or expressed his emotions. I'd never seen him smile. He also never acted up or messed around with boys in class, and during breaks I always saw him sitting at the edge of the classroom, talking with another boy who was around the same height and size. But that didn't mean he was always on his own, or that the other kids didn't like him. More like he was the sort of kid who could have perfect attendance or disappear for a whole month without anyone batting an eye—in other words, he was kind of like Noriko and me.

One night, around a month after Mizuno first spoke to me on my way out of the classroom, he called me on the phone. Luckily, I was right there when it rang. I was about as shocked as I had been the first time that he spoke to me, but I went along with it, switching over to the cordless, then hung up the main phone and went into my room. He led by saying that he had nothing particular to say, but he saw my number in the class directory and figured he'd try calling.

I'd never really had the chance to think about his voice before, and had honestly forgotten what he sounded like, but the voice coming through the receiver sounded strangely deep and muddy, as if the person on the other end of the receiver wasn't actually my classmate, but some other person I'd never met before. The sudden call made me so anxious that I had trouble forming words, and Mizuno hardly said anything at all. After a long, long silence that I was beginning to feel would last forever, Mizuno told me about his day. He'd attended an info session at a college. At the station by the college, he saw his old math teacher, who had evidently transferred to a different school the previous year. I sat on my rug and leaned up against the wall, giving vague responses as the conversation bumped along for about ten minutes, at which point Mizuno said he was going to hang up. I said fine, and while I waited for him to say something else, he actually hung up on me.

After that, Mizuno started calling me on the phone about once a week.

Without either of us picking out a time, it came to be that we talked on Wednesday nights around eight. I was always standing by the phone so I could grab it right away. At first, we both spent lots of time not saying much, but as we got more comfortable, the gaps between what we said grew shorter, and even though we had nothing particular to say, we started slipping jokes into the conversation, even sharing an occasional laugh. Soon enough, I found myself looking forward to our calls, and after about three months, I began to feel an intimacy with him that was different from how I felt about Noriko.

But at school, Mizuno never let on that anything like this was happening.

When we were on the phone, Mizuno would talk about the songs he liked or the novels he'd read, and I would listen, but when I saw him at school he wouldn't even make eye contact with me, much less talk to me. I guess you could say that this behavior was the norm for him, since this was how it was before we started talking on the phone, but the fact of the matter was that our relationship had changed—in however small a way—which made me suspect that he had some ulterior motive. Without fail, he called me every Wednesday night, which made me so confused.

I never told Noriko that I was talking with Mizuno on the phone.

It's not like I promised I wouldn't say anything, but I got the feeling that Mizuno would be unhappy if he ever found out I'd told someone. Besides, Noriko and I had never talked to each other about boys before, so I kept it to myself.

Even over summer vacation, he kept calling as if nothing had changed. Mizuno always called me; I never dialed his number, not once. Toward the end of August, I wound up going over to his house. He said that he had finally tracked down a copy of some rare record and wanted to play it for me.

I switched buses twice and got off at a stop that I'd never heard of. As the bus pulled away, it hit me all at once how far I was from home, which made me feel a little helpless. According to the clock on the cracked wall of the bus shelter, I still had fifteen minutes before he was supposed to be there, so I sat down on a bench with chipping paint and waited for Mizuno. Once the other passengers had walked off in different directions, there was no one around but me.

The flowerbed next to the shelter, the abandoned bicycles, and the asphalt had turned milky white under the brutal summer sun, the entire scene capped off by the hissing of cicadas.

There wasn't a single cloud in the August sky. It was almost painfully clear.

As I sat there surrounded by the blue sky and the whiteness, I felt myself sinking into a depression. A feeling flashed through me, telling me to forget Mizuno and take the next bus home, but I figured that he was probably already on the way here. I turned toward the back of the bench and propped an elbow on the backrest, then closed my eyes and held my forehead up with my palm as my head grew heavier and heavier.

I heard a sound and looked up. It was Mizuno, standing a short distance away, wearing beige slacks and a white polo shirt. There was a big round stain across the chest, which in the light looked like a gaping hole. This was my first time seeing him outside of school. Without his uniform on, he looked like a stranger, a man I'd never met before. But his face was the same as always, the Mizuno I knew from school. Cheekbones a little too pronounced, single eyelids, slightly pointy chin. The hair around his forehead was so damp with sweat that it was getting frizzy. "Irie." When I heard Mizuno's voice call my name, I automatically jumped to my feet. He looked shorter than usual.

We cut down a short shopping street where most of the storefronts were shuttered. Mizuno told me about some of the different businesses. Here's where I used to buy plastic models. Here's where we develop our film. That bookstore belongs to the parents of a kid I went to middle school with. Walking under the increasingly harsh light of the sun, which shone down unobstructed from the highest point in the sky, I gave brief replies to show that I was listening. It was the kind of heat that cups the eyes in darkness. My sweaty feet felt slimy and disgusting in my sandals.

Ten minutes or so into a residential area, the pavement gave way to a dirt road that climbed up a gentle slope. A shrine appeared on the right, and I counted the blue shadows cast by the enormous trees that practically came spilling from the grounds as we walked along. Then we walked under a traffic light that felt strangely out of place and crossed a small stone bridge over an irrigation ditch, leading us into an open area of farmland, greenhouses, and empty lots, where Mizuno pointed up ahead and said his house was over there.

Mizuno lived in the kind of two-story house you see literally everywhere. Out front was a small decorative gate, flanked by flowerpots of different shapes and sizes. Some of them had flowers blooming in them, others had dead grass or just dirt. Mizuno unlocked the door and went inside. I stepped in after him.

When I closed the door behind me, the house went completely dark, and it took a little time for my eyes to adjust. Mizuno told me to go upstairs, then opened a door just beyond the entrance, disappearing down a hall. The buckles on my sandals, usually so easy to unfasten, were stuck. Concentrating on my fingertips, I bent down and tried to see the clasp, but this made the sweat pouring from my body reverse course, rushing toward my face, beads dripping from the tip of my nose to the floor in pitchy splotches.

Upstairs in Mizuno's room, I found one big bookcase and a desk for studying, set alongside a low dresser. Cream-colored curtains hung over the window. The room was small but organized. On his desk were several dictionaries, standing between bookends, and a pencil cup, beside which a big silver alarm clock had been neatly placed. I sat down on a floor cushion that Mizuno brought over from the next room, but Mizuno sat in the chair at the desk, drinking cold mugicha. Ice clattered in the glass, the only sound in the room. The whole house was dead quiet; apparently nobody else was home. His room exuded the smell and heat of a strange house. I was sweating uncontrollably, the polyester fabric of my dress clinging to my lower back and thighs. I saw no AC unit on the wall, so I asked if I could borrow a folder or something to use as a fan. Mizuno slipped a hand between the curtains, opened the window, then handed me a round fan that had been stashed in the bookcase.

A little while later, Mizuno pulled out a cardboard box from under his desk and grabbed the record that he wanted me to see. As I looked over the cover, full of clusters of what looked like hieroglyphs, Mizuno reached out his hand and ran a finger over the designs, explaining how this album was a real collector's item. He excitedly told me about the musicians, who were from Argentina, and the kind of music that they played. I was a little out of it, because I was so nervous and hot, and was distracted by the faintly sour smell of my own breath, which made it hard to talk, but I continued to offer short replies.

Mizuno finished his thought, sipped his mugicha and took a breath, then carefully removed the record from its sleeve, set it gently on the turntable, and lowered the needle. I had no idea what kind of music this was, but it was disturbing. Heavy chords played from some kind of stringed instrument like a wall of waves in the night, emanating from a tangle of sounds. Now and then there was a screech like someone slamming the brakes of a rusty bicycle, while every part of the performance grew more and more eccentric. There was no song, no melody. After a few minutes of listening, I glanced up at Mizuno, who appeared to be overtaken by the music, sitting in his chair with his arms crossed.

As we listened to this noise that he called music, I stared down at the fuzz of the carpet where I had placed my hands and my bag. I imagined a globe in the space between the carpet and me. After taking my time circumnavigating all the different oceans, I found South America, at which point I worked free the narrow wedge of Argentina, like I was pinching out a puzzle piece, flipped it around, then placed it inside other countries on other continents, or sank it into bodies of water I couldn't name, again and again.

The music came to a sudden stop. Mizuno asked me what I thought, but I just nodded a few times.

We listened to the whole album, both sides, multiple times. Mizuno talked about his plans for after graduation, telling me that he was going to take entrance exams at a few universities in Tokyo. Then he walked me through a stack of materials and practice tests that they used at the cram school he'd been attending for the past couple of years. After a little while, he looked at me and asked what I was going to do when school was over.

". . . I think I'll go to college, but I haven't decided yet," I said.

"Isn't it kind of late to be deciding now?" Mizuno asked.

"Yeah."

"But would you go somewhere in Nagoya? If you go."

". . . I guess I don't really see myself in Tokyo," I said. "I mean, almost everybody here who goes to college goes somewhere in Nagoya. Pretty much nobody goes to Tokyo."

"I dunno . . ." Mizuno said after a pause. "I can't stand Nagoya. Everybody at our school gets basically the same grades, so all of those schools will be full of familiar faces. I'll go anywhere but Nagoya. It's not like there's somewhere special I want to be, or something I really want to do, so I guess it doesn't really matter where I go. As long as I don't know anybody there. I've already spent the last eighteen years stuck here." Mizuno looked deep into his hands. "I've had enough of this small town and the way everybody acts here."

I didn't know what to say to this, so I said nothing. Glancing at the clock on his desk, I saw that it was almost three.

"What really matters is how much of this I can get rid of . . . all these things that were decided for me," Mizuno said, fixated on his hands. Beams of sunlight filtering through the curtains lit his body from behind as his face dipped into shadow.

"I didn't choose any of this. Not my family, not my house, not my parents, not my school. This town is overflowing with things I never wanted. But everyone goes around with blank expressions on their faces, like they're wearing matching masks or something. It freaks me out. People here confuse boredom and stagnation with peace and safety. I swear, everyone in this town is pretty much a cow. They just huddle together and moo. Eat their grass and sleep. Then they have babies, and it starts over again. People spend their whole lives like that, never even thinking. It freaks me out . . . Once I get to Tokyo, I'm going to change everything about myself, maybe even my name."

I replayed inside my head what Mizuno had just said. The light spilling over the carpet had shifted slightly toward the center of the room, its color somehow stronger now, larger.

"That's why I need to get out of here. So I can live my life on my own terms, the way I choose. I'll go somewhere I don't know anybody, where nobody knows me, and make a real life for myself. It's like my real life hasn't even started yet."

Mizuno drank the rest of his glass of mugicha and let out a big sigh. For a minute, we just sat there.

"I hope you can make it to Tokyo," I said after a while.

This was followed by another awkward silence, but out of nowhere Mizuno stood up and sat down on the floor next to me. Stunned by how quickly it happened, as if it was some kind of dance move, I jumped back, actually lifting off the carpet, and laughed.

"Was that funny?" asked Mizuno, giggling.

"No," I said, shaking my head. "I wasn't laughing . . . I just, uh, made a noise."

"Okay," Mizuno said under his breath, immediately looking serious. After a pause, he put his arm around my shoulder. My entire body tightened up, as if I'd been hit, and I pulled my legs in from the side and spun away, covering my knees with the hem of my dress. I curled into a ball, turning all the way away from him, and braced my shoulders. For a while, we stayed that way, neither of us moving.

We spent so long in that unnatural position that I have no idea how much time actually passed. I wanted to pull away, to throw off Mizuno's arm and make up some excuse, maybe tell him that I had to use the bathroom, and get out of there. But trying to decide what to do next made me so tense that I could almost hear my body cracking as it shrank, to the point where I was unsure which muscles I would need to move to make my arms and legs do what I wanted them to do. It was a strange sensation, like my core had been twisted up as tightly as humanly possible, but also like I was being crushed to pieces.

I could hear Mizuno breathing through his nostrils. The sound was getting louder, but I sat completely still, hugging my knees, and pressed an ear into my arm to get away from the moisture of his breath. Soon enough, I was floating somewhere just above the corner of the room, gazing at the two of us and the four walls that contained us. It was like this sequence from a dream that I was always having, where for whatever reason I would stumble on an image of myself.

Mizuno took his arm from around my shoulder and wrapped both hands around my jaw, tilting my face up and looking right into my eyes. I looked back at him. It occurred to me that I had never seen somebody else's face so close before. For some reason, he almost looked like he was grinning, making me unsure which part of his face I should look at. The tiny cut under his nose, his pores exuding beads of sweat that looked absurdly three-dimensional. Then there was the smell of sour breath, but I wasn't sure if it was his or mine.

He grabbed me by the forearms and pushed me down. Once he had me on my back, he climbed on top of me, spreading out his weight, and pressed his lips against the side of my neck. Then bringing his face down to mine, he kissed me on the lips a few times. I felt myself drifting away, as I watched my own body being pressed flat and Mizuno stacked on top of me, shrinking along with the rest of the room. The version of me left in the room was horribly flat and without depth, no more than a drawing on a piece of cardstock. Once Mizuno had run his hands all over my dress, he put a hand between my thighs and slowly moved it up until it touched my underwear. I heard myself say no. But this only made Mizuno breathe louder, moving up and down as he shook his head. The hand he had between my butt and my underwear was quivering; I closed my eyes, too scared to look at him. I said no again, but it was like he couldn't hear me. He pulled my underwear down to my knees, then used his foot to push it down as far as my ankles, freeing one of the leg holes from my feet. Once he had his pants off, Mizuno planted himself between my opened legs. A moment later, the tip of his penis pressed into me. No, I said again, twisting away from him and pushing at his shoulders with both elbows, but he wouldn't stop. Unsure of where to put it in, he had to check repeatedly, alternating between his finger and his penis, then tried shifting around and sitting back, but none of it was working. Over and over, he dribbled spit onto his fingers and touched me or prodded at me with his tepid penis. After going through this again and again, I felt a burning sensation travel through me and grabbed Mizuno's shoulders. My body made a sound like it was splintering as I felt his penis go inside me. The pain defied comprehension. Imagine a massive axe being sunk repeatedly into the crown of a massive tree, hands being slipped into the crack to tear the tree in half. Overwhelmed by the pain, I yelled for him to stop, but the next thing I knew Mizuno had ejaculated.

I came back from the bathroom to find Mizuno slumped on the floor, hugging one knee, and looking down. Not moving a muscle. The other leg extended through a faint scrap of evening sunlight.

I felt as though now that the heat and the sun had abated, the edges of everything around me had blurred. And while I could still clearly hear the sound of my own heart, it sounded strange to me, as if it wasn't coming from inside, but from some other place altogether.

From where I stood by the door, I listened to this sound and let my gaze fall on the dresser or the desk or Mizuno's legs, tracing each of these things in my mind. I heard a crow caw somewhere in the distance. A gust of wind blew through the curtains, sending a strange mass of stillness out the door. Mizuno sat there in the same position, not moving for a very long time. Neither did I.

"I need to get home before it gets dark," I said. I sounded weirdly hoarse. Somehow it reminded me of my mother's voice. I took a deep breath, paused, and let it out slowly, so that it didn't just come bursting out of me. In no time, the sun was hanging low in the sky, getting heavier, while the occasional gusts of wind carried a hint of night.

"I'll go with you," Mizuno said, squeezing the words out, his face still buried in his arms.

"It's okay," I said a moment later.

Mizuno took a deep breath through his nose, raising his face a little, then looked down again.

I picked up my bag, sitting on the floor by Mizuno. When I did, he told me he was sorry, barely loud enough to hear.

". . . Earlier," I said, "you were saying you wanted to go to Tokyo . . . so you could make your own decisions."

I spoke slowly, deliberate in my articulation of each word.

Mizuno nodded a few times, his forehead pressed against the arm holding his knee.

"So, what just happened . . . which one was that?"

"Which what?" Mizuno looked up at me and asked.

"Was that one of your decisions?"

"Decisions?" he asked, looking right at me. I looked right back at Mizuno. In my head, I knew exactly what I wanted to ask him, but I wasn't able to find the words to get my point across. Even so, I couldn't keep quiet. The words came out of my mouth on their own.

Mizuno frowned. "What decisions?" he said, sharpening his tone.

"I mean . . ." I managed to say, but it was all that I could get out.

"Do you think there's some connection between what I want to do for college and what we just did?" Mizuno asked, looking aggravated.

"I mean, that's why I'm asking you."

"You mean? You mean what? I have no idea what you're trying to say," he said, scowling. "Know what? I take back my apology," he said after a pause. "You chose to come over, and you were part of what we did, same as me."

I stood there in silence, replaying what Mizuno had said inside my head, over and over. It was true that I came here by choice. I came to his house, took off my sandals and went up to his room. That was what happened.

I left the room and went downstairs to the entrance. The shadows were noticeably thicker than before. Like being underground, I told myself. Mizuno came down behind me.

"Just being around you pisses me off."

Mizuno said this quietly, his words at my back as I put on my sandals.

"You can't think or speak for yourself. You're just going through the motions. I have no idea what you're thinking, when we're at school or when we're on the phone. I guess maybe you aren't thinking at all. It's like there's nothing in there. Just being around you really pisses me off."

As I started walking, a sharp wave of discomfort and pain surged between my legs. Behind me, the cold, quiet evening air was closing in, like it was following me, so I started walking faster, but soon I was off and running. My chest as it rose and fell, the sound of my breath, and my hands and legs swinging back and forth, all of them started feeling less and less real—as if I might float into the air at any moment. No matter how I planted my feet on the asphalt, it didn't seem like they were making contact, but at the same time I was absolutely kicking the ground, while my arms, pale in the twilight, flailed through the chilly air.

I had no idea where I was heading, or what I thought that I was doing. I wasn't even sure that I would ever arrive any-where at all. I ran so hard I thought my body was going to fall apart, and as I listened to the hoarseness of my own breath, I couldn't help but think of Noriko.

After that, the calls from Mizuno stopped, and although we saw each other now and then at school, we never spoke again. The rest of high school passed uneventfully, and I took the exam for a private university in Tokyo that would take me even if my scores were mediocre. And they did. I overheard somebody at school say that Mizuno didn't get into his first choice, but I never heard anything about what happened to him after graduation.

That was the first time and last time I had sex.

7

It hardly rained in August.

I stopped working every evening at six, and drank every day, without exception. When cans of beer and cups of sake were no longer enough, I moved up to the bigger bottles, but after finding out how much cheaper the cartons were when I purchased them online by the case, I began placing regular bulk orders.

Several times a day, I searched for the name Mitsutsuka.

As I drank, I typed his name into the search bar: Mitsutsuka. The only things that ever came up, though, were a place called Mitsutsuka and a profile for a young researcher. No matter how many times I searched but the results were always the same. It wasn't a common name, and the researcher seemed to be some kind of a scientist, so I figured there was some chance that maybe they were related but there was no way to find out, and even if they did, what difference would it make? After clicking through the search results for at least half an hour, I'd admit that I was not going to find the Mitsutsuka I was after— a painful reminder that I didn't even know his full name. I closed the page with a sigh.

When I had nothing to do, I wrote Mitsutsuka's name on a piece of paper. Mitsutsuka, Mitsutsuka . . . with every repetition, the elements of his name broke into separate lines, so that my eyes lost track of what I was writing. I shook my head and drank some sake.

I searched and searched, even though I knew nothing

would come of it. Still, my daily ritual did pay off to some degree. I discovered an arcane expression, "Mikabo no san-zokuame," which uses the same characters as "Mitsutsuka" but in this case pronounces them "sanzoku." The phrase refers to a kind of sudden shower. Evidently there is a Mt. Mikabo in Gunma, and when a thunderhead appears over the peaks, you'll be drenched before you can gather three sheafs ("san-zoku") of wheat. *San-zoku-ame*, I said to myself. I could see it now. The sky goes dark over the mountain, closing in, and then there's a crash of thunder, followed by a vicious rain that drenches the earth with a sound like every sheet of paper in the world being torn. I focused my imagination on the rain, letting it wash away all I could see and all I couldn't see, obliterating everything. Then I imagined Mitsutsuka, standing in the middle of it all, no umbrella over him. I couldn't see his face through the rain. I shook my head and closed my laptop. At the edge of my desk was a stack of galleys that I'd need to begin working on tomorrow. I picked up the one on top and flipped through it. It was a collection of interviews with a famously prolific novelist. Over and over, he said that what he sought to capture in his writing wasn't hopelessness, but hope.

And so the days went by, each one the same. I woke up and worked, then drank from six in the evening. Though I'd never had the strongest appetite, at that point I wasn't eating much of anything, perhaps owing to the summer heat. Pencil in hand, I flagged various spelling inconsistencies with question marks. When a classical text was mentioned, I checked whose translation it was against what the author had said, adding notes where necessary. On recycling day, I brought that week's empties to the trash collection area. My bottles and cans alone filled up the crates set out for everyone to use. One day, Hijiri met me in the neighborhood to give me a present she had bought on her trip to Ko Samui. She said she was sorry for taking so long, that it was just something she bought me at the duty-free, and it had nothing at all to do with Ko Samui. She laughed as she handed me the box. Inside it was a pale yellow bottle of perfume, made by a company called Chloé. I put it back in its box and stuffed it deep into a drawer.

Every time I got in bed, no matter how tired or how drunk I was, I opened the book that Mitsutsuka had given me. The print was small, and while the date listed in the colophon was not so long ago, I smelled old paper every time I turned the page. I brought my nose closer and inhaled deeply. I was finding it difficult to make progress, stopping again and again to let out a sigh. Even when I was fully conscious and giving the book all I had, my mind was dragged into my usual way of reading, eyes gliding over the words, no essential detail finding its way into my head.

Nevertheless, I opened the book and worked my way along each line of text. It talked about large things like the edges of the universe, small things like what we're actually made up of, and delved into hypotheses connecting these separate categories of phenomena—as I read about the special theory of relativity, or the grand unified theory, the sort of things I knew I'd heard or seen someplace before but had a hard time holding onto after reading in a sentence, I did my best to construct some kind of meaning in my head.

Even if I spent all day reading through explanations of electromagnetic waves, light particles as understood by Newton, bands of light created by prisms, dispersion, wave crests, and photons, I saw only the words; none of them stuck even the slightest bit. I fell into a habit of accidentally re-reading the same passage I'd read the night before, and taking far too long to realize it, which soon devolved into reading the same line several times. If I let my guard down even a little, my focus would drift away from the page, and the next thing I knew I was reliving every detail of the first day I met Mitsutsuka, from start to finish, wishing I could fill my world with all things Mitsutsuka and fall asleep.

When would I be able to see Mitsutsuka again?

Once I was finished with the book, maybe I could ask him to meet up, so I could thank him. But I could thank him over the phone. Okay, then how about giving him something in return? No, that felt too aggressive. Maybe it was wrong for me to even think like this. After all, Mitsutsuka and I weren't connected in any way. He didn't lend me this book. He gave it to me. But what did it mean? The book was open in my lap, but these were the thoughts that filled my mind, appearing and then disappearing, unrelated to the content of the book.

Night ended, morning came, and as I looked out on the blueness spreading into the corners of the sky, I thought about what Mitsutsuka had told me, about all the light that was there and yet impossible to see. I worked all day until the twilight snuck up on me, another day like all the others turning into night.

In the sound of the shower or the tub, in the spray of water on the dishes in the sink, I heard the words that Mitsutsuka and I had shared, as well as all the words that we were yet to share. We'd only met up a handful of times, which made it harder to understand how I could feel like this. I didn't know the first thing about him. I couldn't even see inside my feelings far enough to know what they meant. Over and over, I asked myself if this had all been some kind of mistake. If I sat down with a cup of sake and thought about how weird it was that I spent so much time thinking about someone I didn't even know, I just wound up thinking about him anyway. I thought about him all the time.

Sometimes I heard Hijiri's voice telling me that everything was derivative. Sadness and happiness are all experienced by someone else before us; we're simply following their lead. I thought about the kinds of pens that Mitsutsuka carried in the pocket of his shirt, the shapes of all the different caps, then thought about his broad forehead and the way his hair swept off to the sides, or the angle of his hand holding his cup of coffee. I could even recall the contours of his fingernails, as I saw them in that moment. The scar at the corner of his eye, a flake of dead skin that fluttered on his lip when he breathed. Things that I was certain I hadn't noticed at the time, things that probably hadn't even happened, and things I never imagined I'd remember sprang up and multiplied like wildflowers, growing silently and with incredible speed, filling my eyes and ears and heart.

* * *

One of my old bosses passed away. I heard the news from Kyoko.

It was the final week of August. Kyoko told me she was thinking about going to the wake and asked me, with a sigh, if I was going to go. He and I weren't especially close, but he was one of the few people there who showed me anything like kindness. I told her I'd see her at the wake, asked for the time and place, then hung up.

Spotting me out front, Kyoko called me over and we walked in together, while the monk was chanting. We were directed to two seats in the back row, then waited for our turn and went up to burn incense. I put my hands together and closed my eyes, bowing while I remembered my old boss smiling. As we were leaving, we ran into a few former coworkers, but I didn't really say much. Kyoko approached them with her handkerchief held to her mouth, exchanging bows and some softly spoken words.

I was waiting at the edge of the lobby for Kyoko, so I could thank her and say goodbye, but she came over to ask what I was doing after this. When I told her I was probably just heading home, she said we should go somewhere and have tea. We left and walked around for a while looking for a spot, settling on a chain coffee shop just down the street.

"I know they said it was a heart attack, but . . ." Kyoko sighed. "It was probably suicide."

"You think so?" I asked.

"Well, there's no way to be sure," Kyoko admitted, scratching at her eyebrow. "That's just the sense I get, listening to his wife and everything. My uncle killed himself. It's pretty common to say it was a heart attack."

After we had ordered our iced tea, we both fell silent, each of us preoccupied with our own thoughts.

"I mean, he wasn't much of a talker," Kyoko said eventually.

"Yeah, that's true," I said, nodding.

"Thinking about it now, I guess he always seemed a little depressed . . . But what can you do, right? If someone's going to die, they're going to die, right?"

Kyoko was even heavier than the last time that I saw her, which was a few years back, thicker and bigger overall. The armpits of her black dress were dark with sweat. Beads of sweat clung to her forehead as well. Fanning herself with her hand, she craned her neck around, as if trying to locate the AC, and commented again about how hot it was while she pressed her oshibori against her forehead.

"When was the last time we met up?" Kyoko asked.

I said it was a while ago.

"Three years? Four? I can't remember," she laughed. "I know I said I'd give you a call, but things got so crazy at the office that I never got it together, which is a real shame after you helped me out like that. I know, there's no excuse, but I didn't forget."

"No," I shook my head. "It's literally fine."

"Hey, looks like somebody could use a proofreader,"

Kyoko teased. "I guess no one gets hung up on that one any-more, but I remember when 'literally' had a literal meaning."

"Right," I nodded.

"Anyway, who cares? Well, I guess we do. Oh, I know this isn't really the best time for it, but I wanted to give you this."

Kyoko pulled a little box out of her tote bag and set it in the middle of the table. It was wrapped in fancy blue paper.

"Just my way of saying thanks. I could have sent it to you, I know, but I figured I'd bring it along, since we were meeting up."

"Oh, but you've already done so much for me," I said. "You're the one who helped me get the work I'm doing now. If anything, I'm the one who should be thanking you."

"I'm glad to hear it worked out," Kyoko said, smiling with every muscle in her face. "I never had a chance to follow up, but I heard that things were going well. And you're freelance now?"

"That's right," I nodded.

"It isn't much," Kyoko said, pointing at the blue box on the table. "I was worried it might be too girly, but I figured you can never have too much of this stuff. I hope you like it."

I nodded again, debating whether unwrapping it in front of her was the proper thing to do in this situation, then thanked her in a quiet voice as I ran a finger over the wrapping paper.

"It's nothing worth opening here, so feel free to wait until you get home."

"Okay," I said, nodding. When I thanked her again, Kyoko told me I should just put it away, so I bowed as I placed it care-fully inside my bag.

We poured liquid sweetener into our iced teas, stirring with our straws. I drank mine in silence for a while.

"By the way, how's Ishikawa doing?"

"You mean Hijiri?"

"Right, right. Hijiri."

Kyoko opened her eyes wide and snapped her fingers louder than any snap I'd ever heard before.

"I haven't seen much of her lately," Kyoko said. "How's she doing? I mean, without even asking, I'm sure she's doing fine. I remember hearing from her once, around the time you started. Is she still your point person?"

"Yeah, I've been working with her the whole time."

"Wow. You two are pretty much the same age, right?"

"Yeah, the same, actually."

"No kidding. But you're completely different people, which I'm sure has had a lot to do with why the two of you have kept at it so long."

Kyoko took her first sip of tea and carefully wiped her fingertips with the oshibori on the table by her glass.

"Ishikawa's always getting herself into trouble," she said, sighing as if to show her reluctance to discuss this. "She always knows what to say, and she's a great worker. She tells it like it is, no matter who she's dealing with, never compromising on any front, and if that weren't enough, she's gorgeous. She's so pretty that people really listen when she talks. No one can say anything back to her. Despite that, or maybe because of it, she's always getting into trouble."

"What kind of trouble?"

"We work with a lot of the same people. Subcontractors and people like that. And what they always tell me is, well, not that she's trouble, but she's difficult to work with. Impossible, really. They don't want to have anything to do with her."

"Seriously?"

"Seriously," Kyoko answered, not sounding serious at all. "She's a real piece of work. She seems to be fundamentally convinced that everyone is capable of working at her level. So when she sees people around her coming up short, she thinks they're just being lazy. She needs everyone she works with to have standards as high as her own, maybe even higher. But who can put up with that? Everyone's different, with different motivations and approaches to their work. Anyway, it can be really draining to work with someone like that. Who wants to be on edge all the time? That's what people say when they're venting to me, or—you know—at me."

"Really?"

"What about you?" Kyoko asked with expectation in her eyes. "It hasn't been like that for you?"

"Like that . . ." I said, repeating Kyoko's choice of words. I didn't answer right away, since I'd never thought of it that way before, but I said what came to mind, as honestly as I could.

"I've never thought about it."

Kyoko looked at me for a moment, then raised her eyebrows and turned away. She grabbed her straw and took another sip of her tea.

"Then again," she said, wiping her fingertips with the oshibori once more, "maybe your personality's the problem here."

"Problem?" I asked.

"Maybe not a problem. More like a point."

"A point?"

"You know," she said, giving me another long look. "It's fine for someone like you, who never really speaks up. Don't take this the wrong way, okay? I'm saying that's a really good thing. There are lots of people who want to put themselves out there, competing for the spotlight, which makes more problems for the rest of us. But you don't have to worry about that, because you're not like that. And that's the sort of person Ishikawa tends to take on. Take on—or maybe take advantage of."

"Okay . . ." I nodded, even though I couldn't really comprehend what she was saying.

"In short," Kyoko said, "people like her use people like you to validate themselves. Someone like Ishikawa isn't satisfied with forcing everyone around her to accept her approach, or her way of seeing things. She has to push the envelope, every single day. She may be an extreme example, but I guess, to some degree, all people have a deep-seated need to speak their minds and put their thoughts into words. Just think about how advice usually works. People ask for advice all the time, right? But they're not actually asking for somebody's opinion, or what that person would do in a similar situation. Far from it. What they're really doing is putting their thoughts or their own experiences into words. That's why advice never solves anything. Have you ever heard about advice leading to a resolution? Putting things into words like that only adds to the list of problems. It just makes things more complicated. That's what I'm saying, though. Ishikawa knows how to use someone like you, a sponge who sucks everything up without saying anything, to make herself feel big. She's the epitome of that type of person, all too happy to have someone listen to her talk about her wonderful thoughts and views, because it makes her stronger by the day. But not everybody can go along with that, right? They're too busy for it, too grown up. Besides, they don't give a crap about Ishikawa or her ambitions. So they head for the hills. But that's not just because of her personality. The real problem is that she doesn't even realize how blessed she is. She thinks everyone starts out just like her. She's convinced that anyone can succeed with enough effort and determination. You've got to be kidding, right? Some people can speak their minds, others can't. Not exactly a major discovery, I know. And Ishikawa isn't the only one. All the go-getters like her, they put so much pressure on the women around them."

"Pressure?" I asked. "Hijiri?"

"Oh yeah. She's convinced all the men, and all her peers, that the women in the office need to live up to her example and look pretty while they're at it. Like that's part of the job. Women like her are quick to tell you that they never flirt with the men around them, but they absolutely do. They just don't realize they're doing it."

I nodded several times, my eyes falling around Kyoko's chin. As she went on, she spoke faster and faster.

"And that's why—and I know I'm jumping around here— if you get the feeling like she's being extra kind to you, it's probably because she seriously needs you around. She needs someone there to listen, to hear her out. It's all about her. I mean, outside of work, of course."

I drank my water.

"Hey, I hope you know I don't have anything against her. I'm just talking about her reputation, as objectively as I can. I'm only looking out for you, okay?"

I answered vaguely, nodding.

"And one other thing," Kyoko said, slowly stirring the ice with her straw. "I know it's beside the point, but she's got a real appetite for men."

"Appetite?"

"Oh yeah." Kyoko snickered and leaned in a little closer. "She has no self-control. She'll sleep with anybody like it doesn't even matter. Men from work. Guys she met the day before, or even that day. No problem. Well, that's the rumor. Except the rumors are true. I even know a guy who . . ." Kyoko pushed back her chair a little so she could lean in even closer. "Fell into her web."

"Really?"

"Yeah. And she doesn't think there's anything remotely wrong with it. That's what makes it so scary. It's like she has no concept of other people's feelings. I mean, she's one of the beautiful people. That's how she is, from her head to her toes, so I guess there's no surprise there. She puts on a whole show for the men, too, making sure they don't get intimidated or scared off. She dials down her usual assertiveness and all that. But if I were a guy, I'd never sleep with her. No way," Kyoko said, squinting for effect, then shook her head. "If she's even a little curious about a guy, she'll sleep with him and be done with it. The end. And when there's a woman she doesn't like, someone who threatens her position or her pride, she'll steal the man the other woman's after and sleep with him first. Maybe she thinks it's some kind of game or something. She'll seriously sleep with anybody. She does it all the time, and she always has. Makes sense that someone like that has no friends, right?"

"You think so?"

"Sure. She's always alone. When she's not with some guy, I mean. Maybe it looks like she's having the time of her life, but she doesn't look that happy, does she?" Kyoko shook her head and smiled ruefully. "Look, just be careful, okay?"

I said something noncommittal and directed my attention to her fingertips.

Kyoko drank the rest of her iced tea and looked at her watch.

"Ready to get going?"

I nodded and said sure.

"Thanks for today . . . I wish it could have been under better circumstances, but I'm glad we could spend some time together. It really cheered me up. And I finally got to give you your present."

We gathered our bags, stood up, and walked over to the register, where I pulled out my wallet and asked her to let me pay, since last time it had been her treat.

". . . That's right! Okay, thanks for the tea."

The second we stepped outside, Kyoko told me that she was headed the other way. As she lifted a hand to wave goodbye, she said that she was seriously swamped, and had to rush back to do some work. Thanks for everything, I said. Oh hey, she said, as if she'd just remembered something.

"Do me a favor? Don't tell Ishikawa what I said today,

okay? She doesn't need to know. This stays between you and me. I mean, I know I'm the one who introduced you two, but if I'm being honest, I do my best to avoid her. Take care, okay?"

With these parting words, Kyoko crossed the big street and was gone.

When I got home, I opened the present from Kyoko. It was perfume, the exact same kind that Hijiri had given me.

8

H ave a seat," Mitsutsuka said, smiling at me as if we had planned to meet.

I said hello as I pulled out a chair and bowed.

The scene behind my eyes went loose, along with the muscles of my face. It's fine, the alcohol will help, I assured myself several times in my head. You've got alcohol in you, and there's nothing to worry about. When I sat down and our eyes were more or less level, it hit me all at once that I was looking at Mitsutsuka. I said his name again inside my head, *Mitsutsuka*, then worried that I might have actually said it out loud.

"It was 98 degrees yesterday. It's supposed to be around 86 today," Mitsutsuka said. He closed the book that he was holding and looked out the window. "But it's going to get hotter again, starting tomorrow."

"It's September—thunder season," I said. I was so drunk that even I wasn't sure what I'd meant by this, but Mitsutsuka nodded in agreement.

"I really like it," I said. "Thunder, I mean."

"Yeah," Mitsutsuka said. "What would you like?"

"Iced tea."

A minute or so later, the man with the full beard, whom I recognized from last time, came over and stood beside our table. Mitsutsuka ordered an iced tea for me, and when the man asked him if he would like more coffee, he said yes with a bob of his head.

"Sorry, you were saying something," Mitsutsuka said. "About thunder."

"It's thunder season," I said.

Sure is, Mitsutsuka said, then drank what was left of his coffee.

"Thank you for the book," I said. "It was pretty hard, but I understood some of it. I read it before going to bed."

"I'm glad to hear it."

Mitsutsuka had called me ten days after I emailed him.

It had taken me a month, but I made it through the book he'd given me. I felt the unread pages dwindling in my grip until I finally turned the last page and shut the book. The sound was far louder than it should have been, or at least it seemed that way. The following day, once I had finished work and spent a little time drinking and doing nothing, I climbed into bed only to realize that I had no way to occupy myself, which gave rise to an unspeakable loneliness, although I had no idea what it was that made me feel so lonely.

I knew I couldn't contact Mitsutsuka without a good reason, but occasionally it did cross my mind that I could get away with sharing a few thoughts about the book. Over the course of three days, I gathered some observations into an email, which I polished to a diamantine sheen, then spent two more days reading over, until I had some drinks and clicked send with abandon. Mitsutsuka didn't write back. I became incredibly depressed when I realized that there was no truth at all in the words "We regret the things we don't do more than the things we do."

With that in mind, I was so shaken when Mitsutsuka called me that I was unable to answer. As the phone continued to ring, I stamped my feet and spun around in circles, but as soon I realized it had stopped, I immediately called him back. Mitsutsuka said that he had hoped to respond via email, but that he'd been unable to log on.

Was his computer broken? No, his computer was fine, the

problem was his internet provider, a new company that had bugged him so much that he finally switched over, except now he couldn't properly connect. Since he had no clue when it would be up again, he figured he'd call, at least to thank me for the message. Thank you, I said, bowing over the phone, then realized that my mouth was dry as dust.

Mitsutsuka went on to say that my detailed response had made him want to give me something else. It's a CD, he said. I asked if it was classical music. It is, he said. There's a piano piece by Chopin I want you to hear. His lullaby, "Berceuse." I said that he was being too nice to me, first giving me the book, now this. He had to let me do something to show my gratitude. How about you buy me a coffee sometime, Mitsutsuka said with a laugh. I'd be happy to, I said. He said that he was almost always at that same cafe on Thursday afternoons. Alright, I said. Then we hung up.

Pressing my silent phone against my ear as hard as I could, I tightened my entire body and emptied out my lungs.

"Did school start?" I asked.

"It did."

"But you don't need to go to school today?"

"I'm not in charge of a specific class, so I don't have to go in unless I'm teaching."

"Oh, okay."

Shortly thereafter, Mitsutsuka's coffee arrived with my tea. I took the straw out of its paper sleeve and pushed it through the ice cubes filling my glass. As I stirred the straw, watching the light refracting through the glass and ice, I talked with Mitsutsuka. We were discussing light.

"So when I'm reading in my room," I said.

"Right."

"It's night, so I turn on the light, and the room gets bright."

"Right."

"And I can read everything on the page."

"Right."

"Then, when I turn off the light, everything goes dark."

"Yeah," he said.

"Just like that."

"Yeah."

"So all the light that was there when the power was on, where's it go?" I asked. "I mean, it has to go somewhere, right?"

"It's absorbed," Mitsutsuka said. "Most light is absorbed by objects and disappears."

I looked at him.

"It just disappears?"

"Not all of it. Some of it gets reflected, but eventually it's going to run into something, and when it does, it gets absorbed. In the end, it disappears, yes."

"Wow."

"Yeah. But it's possible for some part of the light that doesn't get absorbed to escape, maybe through a window."

"You mean an open window?"

"No," Mitsutsuka said, shaking his shoulders as he laughed. "It's not like that. It doesn't hop out the window or anything. It passes through it."

"Passes through."

"That's right. And some of it keeps going, up into space."

"Into space?" I spoke slowly, one word at a time. "That far?"

"Yeah."

"From my bedroom, into outer space . . ."

"That's right."

"You mean some of the light from my bedroom is some-where out in space, right now?"

"It could be," Mitsutsuka said. "As you know, light travels very, very quickly. Fast enough to travel around the planet seven and a half times per second, so even if the light were to continue without getting absorbed, after all that reflection and transmission, it would go undetected to the human eye. Besides . . ."

"Yeah?"

"In the end, it's going to have to get absorbed."

"So no light lasts forever?"

"Right."

"It all disappears?"

This brought about a period of silence. Both of us looked out the window, absentmindedly observing the people going by. When I looked up, I saw a light fixture not far above Mitsutsuka's head, the bulb glowing under a short black shade.

I checked the time. It was a little after five.

"Before I forget . . ." Mitsutsuka pulled something flat from his bag and set it on the table. It was in a wrinkly yellow plastic bag.

"It's a really good album. I think you'll like it," he laughed.

"I wonder if I'll get it," I said. "I've never really listened to classical music."

"You'll get it. It's just music. Give it a listen, you'll see."

Right, I said, then thanked him and bowed.

"The first piece on the album really reminds me of light."

"Reminds you of light?"

"It does," he said. "It's really beautiful. People don't seem to discuss it very much, but it's my favorite piece by Chopin."

"Wow." I nodded as I touched the wrinkles of the yellow plastic bag with my fingertips.

"There are lots of kinds of light, but what kind do you like?" Mitsutsuka asked after a pause.

"Why did you make that face earlier?" I asked, a little out of it, but saying what had been on my mind. "Were you embarrassed?"

"Whoa, hold on," he laughed. "One dimension at a time."

"Dimension?" I asked, tilting my head to the side.

"If you answer a question with another question, it opens up a different dimension. That's not okay. Unless, well, the second question is contained within the first."

"Okay."

"Anyway, I hope you like it."

Mitsutsuka coughed once and had a drink of water.

"By the way, are there any pianists you like?" he asked.

"No, none," I replied. "I mean, it's not that I don't like them. I've just never really listened to, you know, real piano music. I can't think of a single pianist."

"Not even the really famous ones?"

"Not even the really famous ones."

"Really?" Mitsutsuka asked. "What about Argerich? I feel like a lot of women listen to her."

"No, I've never heard of her."

"What about Glenn Gould?"

"I know the name," I said. "Is it Glenn Gould playing on this CD?"

"No, this one's a Japanese pianist."

"Oh, okay."

"As a matter of fact, Gould hated Chopin," Mitsutsuka said. "His performances were only ever about one thing: humanity. The human condition. Nothing about light or anything else. I like Gould, but as I get older, I find myself less and less interested in listening to him."

"The humanity's too much for you?"

"Something like that." Mitsutsuka laughed. "Though I think a lot of people feel that way. It's not the only reason, but he kind of wears me out."

After that, Mitsutsuka told me about how Glenn Gould was a serious dog lover, and how his dogs tended to have far more memorable faces than Gould himself, and how one time on stage, Gould grew so distracted by the dog hair on his suit he set about removing it using a piece of tape or something, even though the orchestra was mid-performance.

There was nobody in the cafe except for us, and it didn't seem like anyone was going to come in anytime soon. The mysteries of light remained central to our conversation. My part in the discussion was mainly listening to Mitsutsuka talk, but if I tilted my head, he'd notice and take the time to explain. He even took his notebook from his bag, opening to a blank page to illustrate a point for me. While I listened to Mitsutsuka talk, I observed the length of his fingers around his pen, or the tone of his skin, then look at the pens in his shirt pocket, and watch his eyes trained on the page, and the brown spots in the skin around them. Beads of sweat were forming across his forehead; I discovered that he had a tiny mole just above one of his eyebrows. As Mitsutsuka walked through the niceties of the illustration he had drawn, tapping at it with the tip of his ballpoint pen, I hummed along to his explanation, relaxing into the rhythms of his voice.

"Okay. Now it's your turn to draw something."

I was almost in my own world when Mitsutsuka said this out of nowhere, as if he thought this was a great idea. He handed me his pen and turned the notebook to a fresh page.

"Me?" I was flustered at being put on the spot like this, but I took the pen and muttered to myself. "What should I draw?"

"Anything you like," Mitsutsuka laughed.

"But I can't draw. I can't even draw a pie chart."

"Alright."

Mitsutsuka stared at the hand I was about to draw with. The thought that Mitsutsuka had his eyes on me made my back grow hot, and that heat spiraled up around my neck, finally collecting in my cheeks before spreading through my entire face.

"I don't know what to do."

"Just draw something, anything you want," Mitsutsuka said.

". . . Is it okay if I write something?"

"Sure."

"Okay, what should I write?"

"Anything."

"Anything at all?"

"Okay, what about a word you've never written down before?"

"Hmm," I nodded, unsure what else to say. A word I'd never written before—no matter how hard I thought, none came to mind. For a moment, I thought about writing "putrefaction," but I wasn't sure I could spell it without making a mistake.

"Can I write something else?"

"Of course."

"Okay."

Then I wrote down my name and address.

"Hey, this is some nice handwriting," Mitsutsuka said, holding the notebook a short distance from his face. It sounded like he was genuinely impressed.

"It's really not," I said quietly. "It's finicky, I don't know . . ."

"You think so? I think it's beautiful," he said.

No idea how to respond to this, I shook my head over and over.

* * *

Soon I was spending most of the day listening to the Chopin lullaby that Mitsutsuka had given me. I downloaded the track and played it on repeat while I worked at my computer, and when I got up from my desk, I plugged my earphones into an old CD player I'd managed to find in the closet. Although I couldn't listen to the lullaby in the bath, I had it playing almost every minute I was at home, even when I was cooking or eating.

The album that Mitsutsuka gave me contained piano music by several composers, but I listened to the Chopin lullaby exclusively. The cover featured a photo of a pianist still in his youth, playing the piano against a background of navy blue. Just like Mitsutsuka said, the melody was full of the qualities of light, as if pointing gently toward something, or guiding something along, each sound twinkling through the veil of darkness that surrounded me when I closed my eyes. In my chair, I surrendered myself to a world of sound that could only be described as sparkling. It made my head sway, and my breath grew deeper as my legs climbed up that evanescent staircase, each step a sheet of light. They would shimmer to life the second my sole made contact, then fizzle into stardust when I lifted my foot, only to be reborn as yet another step, gently showing me the way. That slowly winding spiral stairway of light ascended freely through the dark, and though I was unsure where it was taking me, or what I would find when I arrived, as long as the music was playing, I knew that there was nothing to fear, that I could go anywhere at all. As I climbed one step after another, I ran the soft part of my finger over every gleaming note, stringing them together in a necklace that I placed over my chest, or stretching them with both hands into a hoop of light that I could step inside and pass through, over and over. I took a giant breath, my utterly transparent chest sparkling with light as if I'd swallowed a nebula from tens of thousands of light years away. My exhalation, sparkling with a mist of light, hovered before me, but if I scooped it up in my hands and took another deep breath, my arms and throat began to glow from the inside, down to my palms, and as I gazed into them, I realized I was floating in space. I shut my eyes and held out my arms, shaking my body and head every which way, dancing and stirring up the light as I waltzed endlessly around my apartment.

Every Thursday, I went to the cafe to see Mitsutsuka.

On rare occasions, there were other customers, but it was usually just the two of us. Mitsutsuka took his time with his coffee, and I tried to drink my iced tea at a comparable pace, not wanting it to mix too quickly with the alcohol that I'd been drinking since the morning. Mitsutsuka had initially insisted that I let him pay, but I proposed we take turns treating one another. I found him there every single Thursday evening, just like he had said I would, and before long we were talking about all kinds of different things.

We were spending about three hours together every week, much of which involved Mitsutsuka telling me all about physics, although I was unable to grasp most of what he said.

One time, when I casually asked him what was the smallest thing in the world, he spent an hour explaining all kinds of things to me, almost like he was talking to a student. He taught me about the elementary particles, which can't be broken down any further, such as quarks and leptons that were further classified into several "flavors," or types. He explained that the number three had a mysterious significance in physics, with quarks and leptons grouped, for reasons no one understands, into three-flavor sets. When I told him I thought that quark was kind of a cute name for a particle, he said I only thought so because of the spelling, and explained that it got its name from how a bird cries three times—"quark, quark, quark"—in a strange novel called *Finnegans Wake*, which was written in English, but includes words from languages all over the world. He also told me about a school of thought according to whom the smallest substances in the universe weren't even shaped like particles, but more like strings, and then introduced me to the idea that there was a chance that all of us are composed of these incredibly tiny strings, which may in fact contain countless dimensions too small for us to ever comprehend. I was so spellbound that all I could do was nod and nod some more.

Mitsutsuka always sat in the same seat, wearing the same tired polo shirt and carrying the same shoulder bag. Its corners were fraying. Mitsutsuka not only lent a kind ear to my silly questions, he even laughed occasionally, as if he was genuinely having a good time.

Sometimes he told me things about the high school where he taught. His school was remarkably advanced in its efforts to address and prevent sexual harassment and abuse of power, to the point where they had been recognized as a model school multiple times. As a result, Mitsutsuka had become well versed in these matters. Evidently every door accessible to students was to be left open at all times, and it was off limits for a student and a teacher to spend any time alone together, on or off campus, or even for teachers to address the students by their first names.

"Really?" I asked, speaking through a mental haze. "That never would have happened when I was a kid."

"It's different now."

"But, I don't know, you're always . . ."

"Yes?"

I almost hiccupped, then continued.

"Always teaching me new things . . . even though I'm obviously too old for high school."

"True," Mitsutsuka laughed.

"But I feel like, since you're always teaching me new things, it's like I'm basically your student," I said, tacking on a little laugh.

"But if you were a student, we wouldn't be able to meet up like this," Mitsutsuka said after a moment.

I looked out the window for a moment, before redirecting my attention to the table. When I took a shallow breath through my nose, the faint smell of sake spread through my nostrils.

"I don't know . . . I guess that's how it feels, for me," I said.

"Except I'm older . . . with nothing ahead of me, and, well, this isn't school."

"That hadn't occurred to me," Mitsutsuka said.

We fell into another period of silence.

"Does it make you uncomfortable?" he finally asked.

"Uncomfortable?" I was so stunned by the word that I said it back.

"I mean, what you just mentioned. Feeling like a student."

"No, it's not that," I said, cueing another silence.

"Alright, as long as you're not uncomfortable," Mitsutsuka said, then took a sip of coffee.

I stared at the wrapping that my straw had come in, now crumpled up on the table. The door opened to a clatter of chimes, and in came a delivery man carrying a cardboard box so large that he could barely see over the top. While the bearded owner signed the slip, the delivery man made some sort of joke and they shared a hearty laugh. The delivery man took the slip and quickly made sure everything was in order, then offered a cheerful cry of thanks and ducked out of the cafe.

"Mitsutsuka?"

"Yes?"

"I guess maybe I am . . . a bit uncomfortable."

I spoke quietly as I watched the door swing closed. After I said it, I detected an ungainly noise rising up my throat and felt my hands close around my neck in an attempt to stop it from spilling out of my body.

"I see," Mitsutsuka said after a pause. "Well, let's take steps to resolve that."

I couldn't look Mitsutsuka in the eye, so I gazed outside for a while, and when I had run out of things to look at, I stared into my glass, the ice now melted, leaving the tea more or less colorless.

"I've got it," he finally said. "I'll stop calling you Ms. Irie. How's that sound, Fuyuko?"

I lifted my head and looked at Mitsutsuka's face.

"I'm not allowed to call my students by their first names, so that'll keep things in perspective."

"Okay."

"Then again, we're meeting up like this, and that's already something that could never happen with a student."

"Yeah."

"Does that sound like a plan to you?"

"Yeah."

"And you've never called me sensei anyway."

"Right."

"If we come up with something better, we'll go with that."

"Okay."

"What do you think? Sound like a plan?"

". . . Okay."

Unable to face Mitsutsuka once again, I hung my head and quietly said okay one last time, then nodded again and again.

Once this was behind us, and Mitsutsuka switched over to calling me Fuyuko, we started to meet up all the time. My weekly trips to catch him at the cafe on Thursday evenings were never scheduled or acknowledged, at least not in a formal way, but before long we'd added Sunday evenings, and I was seeing Mitsutsuka twice a week.

I learned that he was fifty-eight years old, that his birthday was December tenth, that he set a record high score on Space Invaders when he was younger, that there were no foods he especially liked or hated, that he rarely snacked between meals, that he played basketball for a short time in his student days, that he didn't care for folk music, that he was born in Tokyo, that he was five foot seven, that he had never broken a bone, or ever gotten stitches, and that his blood was type A. I told him that I had grown up in Nagano, that my birthday was Christmas Eve, that I didn't go anywhere this summer, that I get a slight headache when I eat anko, that as a kid I'd been hit by a car when riding a bicycle, that I'd missed a school trip once when I had appendicitis, and that there was a little park behind my apartment building. I also told him that I'd never permed my hair, or left Japan, then he told me that his hairline had begun receding in his late thirties. At one point, he did a card trick for me, but I figured out how it worked on the first try. You got me, he said, blushing, and the next time we met up he brought a book with all kinds of magic tricks in it. If our feet happened to bump underneath the table, we both launched into a series of apologies, after which there was a predictable period of silence. All in all, the things we shared might have been childish, but they became the building blocks of a relationship, making me feel as if I'd made some kind of a mark in his memory.

But I knew so few of the things that I really wanted to know about Mitsutsuka. The questions never found their way into words. Not like he made it hard for me to ask. Far from it. I simply couldn't get the words out.

It was so quiet on our way back to the station.

What anyone else would have seen as the normal passage of evening into night was a blue dusk that we moved through as if making our own path, a moment in which Mitsutsuka and I glowed with the same color. Every time, he waved goodbye in the same way, then vanished around the corner, up the stairs. There was always something I wished I could have said, something else I wanted to share with him, but before I could find the words and send them through the air, he was around the corner and gone.

* * *

On the first Monday in October, Hijiri called me up to see how I was doing. Between the Obon holidays and the end of

September, I had received far fewer manuscripts than usual. Turning off the lullaby, I pressed the phone against my ear and nodded at the strength of her voice, realizing it had been a fair amount of time since she and I had spoken.

"Everything's running behind schedule. I was expecting all these manuscripts to come rushing in over the summer, but you know how writers can be! Anyway, it looks like things are going to be pretty busy through October and November, so I might have to ask a lot of you," Hijiri said. "Think that'll be okay?"

As she gave me the schedule for the coming months, I nodded along as I wrote a few notes into my calendar. Once we'd finished talking about work, Hijiri filled me in on how she'd been doing otherwise, but as I listened to her talk, I saw Kyoko before me—the image of her face, and the feeling of her voice from that afternoon so long ago.

"I know you said that you weren't going anywhere this summer," Hijiri said, "but what was September like?"

"I stayed home," I told her.

"You really didn't go anywhere?" Hijiri asked in an exaggeratedly high-pitched voice.

"Really."

"I guess you did say you weren't even going back to Nagano."

"What about you?" I asked Hijiri.

"I dunno, I just did whatever."

"Whatever?"

"Yeah. Did some work, met up with a few people, went out to eat . . . the usual, really."

"What happened with the elephant guy?" I asked.

"Elephant guy?" Hijiri asked. "Oh, him! It's kinda complicated, but we still get together sometimes."

"You do?"

"For a while, I was thinking we should cut it off, but as soon as I started thinking like that, it took all the pressure off. Weird, right?"

"Yeah."

"I'm pretty sure he feels the same way, too. We've got good chemistry—and that helps, but it just feels like it's been dragging on a bit too long, you know?" Hijiri made it sound like it was somebody else's life we were talking about.

"Sounds tough," I said, looking at my calendar, where I'd circled all the dates I'd seen Mitsutsuka at the cafe.

"What does?" Hijiri sounded puzzled. "What I just said?"

". . . I mean, you're busy as it is, but then, like, didn't you say you were seeing other people, too?" I asked, being careful not to speak too quickly.

"Sorta," she said, in a tone that made it clear it was no big deal. "That's not exactly what I would call tough, though." Hijiri laughed. "Not like we're meeting up for work or anything. If I don't want to see them anymore, I'll stop."

"But weren't you saying you don't really like them? That sounds pretty tough—at least to me."

"It's really not, though, seriously."

"Yeah?"

"Yeah. We only meet up when I feel like it."

"Yeah."

"Didn't I say that before? Anyway, what's really bumming me out now is all the money that I've gone through. First the trip, then I bought a full set of skincare products. I got two pairs of these shoes I liked, the same style in different colors. And I know it's a little stupid, but I bought myself another coat when the winter collections came out. Once you get going, it's so hard to stop. Every year, I wonder how long I can keep this up, but I know I'm only doing it because I like it, right? No use fighting it, you know?" Hijiri laughed like she was having fun. "Hey, remember when we went out for drinks a little while back, and I was wearing a cardigan?"

"Yeah, I remember."

"The gray one."

"Yeah, I know the one you mean."

"You want it?"

"What do you mean?"

"Well, you told me how much you liked it. You know, the one with the beads on the chest—that cardigan. I bought another one kinda like it, so I was wondering if you might want that one."

"I mean . . ." I started to speak, but that was all I could get out. I had no idea what I would wear with something so pretty, or when I would even get to wear it. "That's really nice of you, but I don't think it would look good on me."

"Why not?" Hijiri was unconvinced. "Cardigans are cardigans. They don't look good or bad on anybody. You just put them on. That's it."

"But . . ." While I was struggling to come up with an answer, Hijiri said she had a bunch of other stuff that she wanted to send me, that I could keep whatever I wanted and toss the rest. Then she hung up.

9

"ifteen years! Crazy, right?"

Noriko Hayakawa gave me a smile that was almost bashful. We'd seen each other a few times after graduating, but it had been a really long time. It's crazy, I said. I laughed and so did Noriko. That voice really took me back.

"I'm so glad you could meet up," she said. "I know how busy you are."

"Not at all. I was so happy to hear from you."

"I wasn't sure how you'd react . . . I mean, dude, you didn't come to our reunion. That was what—six, seven years ago? I was hoping I'd get to see you there."

"Oh, I'm sorry about that."

Noriko shook her head, then took a look around the restaurant.

"I can't remember the last time I was in Tokyo. Maybe ten years ago? I wish I could say it looked different, but I can't remember anything about the last time I was here."

"That's just the way it is. I feel the same way, and I live here."

"Do you come to this part of town a lot?" Noriko asked. No, I told her, not that often, almost never. Just then, our spaghetti arrived at our table.

"They're fast, huh?" Noriko said, eyes opened wide.

"Uh-huh."

"Harajuku's so crowded. All those heads, they look like those knobby curls on a giant Buddha."

Noriko had sent me New Year's cards every few years—I

guess whenever she remembered—which was how I knew that she had gotten married back in Nagano and had two kids. I'd written back a few times too. This is how we stayed in touch over the years, but we'd never once spoken on the phone. So when she called me the week before, even though her name had popped up on my screen, it took me a few seconds to realize who it was.

"How long are you going to be in Tokyo?" I asked.

"Until tomorrow morning."

Noriko twirled a bit of spaghetti on her fork and took a bite, then made a face like she was surprised by how good it was. "This is amazing. We don't have this chain back home."

"How was Disneyland?" I had a bite of spaghetti and nodded.

"Super crowded. It was everybody's first time, so we had no idea what to do or where to do it, but at least we got to see the parade, which was nice."

It was a bit disorienting to be spending time with Noriko like this, in a place where we had no history.

"Look at how skinny you are." Noriko sounded concerned. "Are you eating enough?"

"Sure," I said with a smile.

"Yeah? As long as that's true. You just look really different is all."

The Noriko in front of me was so much heavier than the Noriko that I remembered. She was almost like a different person. The lace sleeves of her cardigan were unflatteringly tight around her upper arms.

"Hey, check it out. We're still making these." Noriko pinched at the front of her cardigan. There was a cat patch by the hem. "You remember?"

"Of course," I laughed.

"But check you out. I love the look. That sweater must have cost a lot."

"Not really."

I sort of laughed, touching the beads spread across my chest.

"How's everyone at home?" I asked.

"They're doing okay," Noriko said, laughing through a sigh. "Nowadays most of the companies are having their stuff made in China to cut costs. Production is way down from what it used to be. We're barely hanging on. My folks have all but retired."

The windows on the second floor, where we were sitting, opened out onto the crowded streets of Harajuku. People walking down the street, a succession of lit signs in every possible color. I thought about how all the colors I was seeing were the colors that were left behind. Where had the actual colors gone? I knew that Mitsutsuka had explained this to me clearly, and I was disappointed that I couldn't remember it now. Bicycles were crammed together on the sidewalk just below us. I watched a young girl passing by throw a plastic bottle into one of the front baskets.

As we ate our spaghetti, Noriko told me about her life, and I told her about my work as a proofreader. You always did like books, she said to me. Not really, I said. I don't know, that's definitely how I remember you, she said as she spun the spaghetti around her fork and took another bite.

When the coffee arrived after dinner, Noriko let out another sigh.

". . . Anyway, that's where my head is these days. I don't know what to do."

"But you must have some good times too, right?" I asked. Noriko shrugged.

"Good times . . . What's that even mean? When you've been married for ten years, you kinda lose track. Not like complaining helps." Noriko laughed. "I guess that's just the way it is, though. Ten or twenty years of the same thing, every single day, until you can't go any further and that's it—it's over."

"Is there something else you'd rather do?"

"No. But that's not really the point, I guess."

"Yeah."

"Know how I quit my job when I got married and had my first kid? Well, sometimes I'm not so sure that was the best decision. I mean, it was the kind of job I was fine putting behind me, so no regrets there. Someone's got to take care of stuff around the house, and thinking rationally, I guess it made sense for me to be the one to stop working and stay at home with the kids . . . Like, I know it's a little late to say so . . . but not having my own money to use how I want is a real bummer. Oh well, too late . . . Geez, this can't be any fun to listen to. Sorry."

Noriko gave me a worried look and laughed. I shook my head and said I didn't mind.

"I guess it goes without saying, but now that we have a couple of kids, I've become a total mom, and my husband's a total dad. And that's all we are. Know what I mean? It's enough and all, but it's literally who we are. I'm scared to think what it'll be like when the kids are grown, when my daughter leaves the house, what's going to be left of us? Sometimes, we find ourselves alone, just the two of us. Sometimes. When it does, we've got nothing to talk about. Nothing at all. All we ever talk about is the kids. Or maybe something on TV, or our parents."

"Yeah."

". . . Then there's the sex." The way Noriko said this made it sound like it was hard for her to say. "We haven't done it since I got pregnant with our youngest, not once. I can't believe I'm telling you this. Anyway, I guess we just, like, never feel like having sex. It's like it's ceased to exist. At least between the two of us."

I nodded, sending no specific message.

". . . There are all kinds of sexless marriages, though. Like, if one of you wants it, wants to do it, but the other one can't get in the mood, there's still a shred of hope. I know it hurts to be rejected, but you can still talk about it. There's still room to make things better."

I nodded again.

"But with us, both of us have stopped wanting each other that way, and that's a real problem. Sex simply doesn't exist in our home. I've mentioned it to friends, just asking generally what they think about couples who are having trouble in their sex lives, saying that it seems to be a pretty common problem, not letting on it's me, but they were just like, yeah, of course. Like, once you're family, it'd be weird if you had sex. You'd be surprised how many people see it that way, actually. And I guess that's where I've been at for a while now, not giving it much thought, or thinking that it's normal or whatever. But when I really started to think about it, the idea of never having sex with anyone ever again, for the rest of my life, until I die . . . What's normal about that?"

"Yeah."

"What do you think? If you were me . . . Which would you choose?"

"Choose?" I was confused. "Between what and what?"

"You know." Noriko leaned forward, bringing her face closer to mine. "Living out the rest of your life without sex, without excitement, without stimulation, passing your days peacefully as mother to your children, or . . ."

Noriko stopped there. I waited for her to keep going.

"Well," she said, "I guess that pretty much sums up the life ahead of me." Noriko let out an exaggerated laugh. "I mean, this is the life I chose. I asked for this. Maybe we could have done something, as a couple, to keep this from happening. Tried harder, or something. But we didn't."

I nodded several times, acknowledging the argument.

"But, yeah, if I still had a job, and maybe a little money in the bank, I think I'd probably leave him, even with the kids. Trouble is, there's no way child support and a part-time job would be enough. That's no way to live. Besides, the kids haven't done anything wrong. They don't deserve that."

"I mean, I have no idea how single mothers do it . . . working while raising kids on their own."

I said it the second the thought had crossed my mind and watched Noriko tense up, if only for an instant. A couple with a small kid passed our table; the toddler tripped and fell headfirst on the floor and started crying like it was on fire. Noriko glanced over at the family, then back over to the table, taking a deep breath through her nose before continuing her thought, no comment on what I had said a moment earlier.

"My husband's cheating on me," she said.

"Really?" I asked, genuinely surprised.

"That's why nothing's going on at home."

Noriko tore the end off a stick of sugar and poured it into her half-empty cup of coffee, then mixed it in with a few clinks of her teaspoon.

"Does your husband know that, um, you know?"

"Well, he has to know that I know something, but I haven't come right out and told him. I'm sure I could find all kinds of proof, though, if I really wanted to, but I guess I don't have it in me. I know who the woman is, through Twitter. Are you on Twitter? Everybody writes the most mindless, meaningless stuff on there. I thought maybe I could find her, so I looked around, and there she was, using her real name. Like, I can see everything she's doing every day."

"Seriously?"

"People really let their guard down. It's wild. If you just read somebody's tweets, you can find out everything you ever wanted to know about them. Where their parents live, what their kids look like, what their friends are up to, where they're going on their next vacation, everything. I bet it's never even crossed her mind that I'm checking her posts every day."

"Yeah," I agreed.

"Anyway, there's no point in forcing my husband to admit what's going on. It wouldn't change anything."

I nodded.

"Besides, I'm in no position to talk," Noriko said, with a smile in her eyes. "You know how I went to the reunion? Well, I met up with this guy there, got to talking, and it just happened. Not like he was a total stranger . . . But yeah, one thing led to another."

"With someone from our class?" I asked.

"Remember that guy Yoshii? I never really talked to him before, but seeing him there, after all that time, he was so easy to talk to. It was crazy. Like meeting a new person, but not. Reunions are strange that way."

"Does your husband know?"

"Maybe he does, maybe he doesn't. I bet it's the same for him. He knows that facing the facts won't change anything, so we might as well keep going. But something definitely feels off. On some level, it doesn't feel real. I mean, I'm still seeing Yoshii. It's fun. Oh, he's got kids, too. Things are good for him at home, but he's got other problems, and we talk about that stuff a lot—but that's not the point . . . when we're together, we have a good time. I don't love him or want to be with him or anything like that. But the more we meet up, the harder it gets. Every time I see him, I dunno . . . it just gets harder. I mean, it's good when we're together. But after . . . I don't know how to explain it. 'Dead inside' is a little too dramatic. I just feel hard and numb, like some part of me is losing all feeling. I can't stand being alone. I know this is my own doing, but it makes me really sad. It's hard to put my finger on it, but I know it wasn't supposed to be like this."

For a while Noriko was silent, staring at the table.

"And the longer this goes on, the more it feels like it isn't even my own life. Cheating housewives are everywhere. And who cares about people like that, right? What they think, what they do. But at some point, I start seeing myself like that. Anyway, it's meaningless and stupid, so we meet up again. Then I feel bad about it all over again."

Noriko went silent again, eyes on the table.

". . . See, that's the thing. I eventually forget how much it hurts. So I call him up, we see each other, and then it sucks again, in an endless cycle. Sometimes, when I get home and see my husband there, zoned out in front of the TV, I wonder if maybe he's feeling the same as me, like it's all a mess and everything sucks. But the thought of that makes me start to cry. I don't want him to hurt. I just want him to feel okay. I don't want him to feel the way I'm feeling, you know?"

For a while we just sat there, staring out the window. Noriko broke the silence.

"I can't believe I told you all that. I haven't even seen you in years. We probably should have talked about something more fun, like, I dunno, the stuff we used to talk about." She stretched and shook her head lightly. "Sorry."

"It's fine, honestly," I said. "This is important."

"I appreciate it. Anyway, I'm sure that this sounds really bad, but I love having kids. They're the best. I feel like they're all that keeps me going, seriously."

"Yeah," I said.

"I don't know what it is. It's like you're not even there anymore, like your life just vanishes. It's all about the kids. Nothing else matters, I swear. There's so much you can learn from them, too." Noriko beamed. "Are you ever going to have kids?"

"Kids?"

"You should think about it. You should definitely have kids," Noriko said, trying to sound persuasive. "It's not something you're thinking about?"

"No."

Oh, that's too bad, she said, almost talking to herself as she finished off the last of her coffee, you'd be an amazing mom.

I continued staring out the window.

". . . I haven't told anyone else about our, you know, situation," Noriko said a little later. "I haven't even mentioned it to Yoshii. Not a word to anyone—not to the other moms, or my friends back home. You're the first."

"Wow."

"I wonder why it was so easy for me to tell you," Noriko said. "I guess because you're not one of the main characters in my life anymore . . ."

Noriko looked at me and grinned.

"If you were, I don't think I could have said anything."

For a moment, neither of us said a word. As we sat in silence, the clamor of the restaurant hit me all at once. Kids crying at tables all around us, someone with a phone pressed against their ear and laughing loudly, a group of college kids talking on and on with incredible energy. A waitress reading back an order in a shrill voice, the ceaseless ringing of the electronic bell that guests use to call the server. Hearing all the sounds filling the space around us, we decided it was time to leave. We got up with our bags, each paying our part of the bill at the register. As we were about to go down the stairs, Noriko said something that had evidently just occurred to her.

"Hey, that guy died."

I turned to look at Noriko.

"I heard at the reunion. You know, that guy . . ." Noriko pressed her lips together, struggling to remember his name. "What was his name . . . Ugh, what was it?"

Speechless, I stared at Noriko's frowning face.

She returned her wallet to her bag and stood there, pressing her fingers over her eyelids, saying come on, what's his name, over and over. I could hear my pulse beating around my ears.

"Got it!" Noriko yelled, looking me in the eye, visibly

pleased. "Koga! His name was Koga. I never really talked to him, but you probably remember him, right? He died, from lung cancer, maybe six years ago."

Koga, I said under my breath, but I remembered nothing, not the name and not a face to put it to. I let out all the air in my lungs.

"Wow," I said.

"Unbelievable, right?" Noriko said. "It doesn't matter how young you are. Once it's in your lung cells, that's it, you're done."

As we walked down the stairs, she looked back several times, giving me all the details about how Koga had died, Koga from our old class, Koga who was nowhere in my memory.

Noriko said that she had to meet her husband and their daughter here in Harajuku, then raised a hand to say goodbye. I told her to take care. When we said goodbye, I couldn't help but feel like there was something else that I should say to her, but all I could do was lift my hand up to my chest and give a little wave. As I watched Noriko get smaller, going off into the distance, I had a hard time believing that the person I was watching from behind was the same person I had spent all that time eating dinner with and talking to. At this point, I was no longer able to recall what Noriko used to look like, the Noriko I knew in high school. All that remained was a faint shred of her voice, frail like it was trembling in the wind, as we walked side by side, Noriko always to my right, in the empty hours that we spent together before and after school, dressed in identical school uniforms, but now that wispy voice was being eclipsed by the face of a grown woman who was prone to sighing and wearing brown lipstick, her fleshy chin resting on the back of her hand, everything slipping further into the distance with each blink, with every second.

I waited until Noriko had disappeared completely into the crowd of people crisscrossing the street before I walked away, which was when I saw a young guy trying to extract his bicycle from the row of bikes. He gripped the handlebars and pulled the bicycle free, making a lot of noise, and clicked his tongue when he saw his basket, which was full of plastic bottles like it was a trash can. He tossed the bottles into the basket of the bike next to his, the same bike I had seen from upstairs. When he realized I was staring, he asked me what the hell I was looking at and called me an ugly bitch.

I walked from there to Shibuya.

The forecast said it would be cloudy, but on the way it started to rain. Some of the people around me pulled collapsible umbrellas from their bags, making me feel as if I must have heard it wrong, that it was supposed to be a rainy day after all. The rain fell hard for just a few minutes before turning into more of a mist. I was just about to enter the station when I saw the train taking off, so I stood at the corner of a large intersection and watched the endless waves of people.

I'm all alone, I thought.

I'd been on my own for ages, and I was convinced that there was no way I could be any more alone, but now I'd finally realized how alone I truly was. Despite the crowds of people, and all the different places, and a limitless supply of sounds and colors packed together, there was nothing here that I could reach out and touch. Nothing that would call my name. There never had been, and there never would be. And that would never change, no matter where I went in the world. Surrounded by the grayness of the city, ever grayer in the misty rain, I was unable to move.

I have no idea how long I was standing there like that, but I eventually started walking, boarded a train, and got off at the station near the cafe Mitsutsuka always went to. There was no other place for me to go, no home for me to return to, no street that I could follow any further. It was a Monday. I found this reassuring, since Mitsutsuka probably had class. I couldn't bear him seeing me this way, with nothing to drink, a total mess. All I really wanted was to stand outside and see the seats where he and I always sat together.

I pushed through the familiar turnstiles and walked down the street to the cafe, saying his name inside my head, Mitsutsuka, but then I felt an intense pain in my throat. My chest felt so tight it stopped me in my tracks. *Mitsutsuka*. It kept on coming. *Mitsutsuka, Mitsutsuka*. Repeating his name, I walked with my head down through the drizzling rain. When I arrived at the cafe, I looked up and saw Mitsutsuka standing outside.

"Fuyuko?"

Mitsutsuka was holding an umbrella, standing in the rain.

The dark blue umbrella threw a pattern of light blue spots on his broad forehead. It was Mitsutsuka. As I stood there unable to speak or even move, Mitsutsuka said my name one more time. Fuyuko. He was gripping the handle of his umbrella, standing a few yards away. Mitsutsuka was looking at me, a little surprised. I stood there, looking back at him. But almost immediately I closed my eyes tight, scrunching up my nose, eyelids, and eyebrows with as much force as I could muster. I gritted my teeth and grabbed the strap of my bag with both hands, squeezing my eyes shut with all the power I had in me. Heat flared through my nose as I struggled to keep my trembling eyelids shut, sensing that the slightest movement would bring a flood of tears. I was unable to take a breath or let one out.

"Fuyuko, you're soaking wet."

Mitsutsuka sounded closer than before. I nodded again and again, without opening my eyes. Although I hadn't seen it happen, I could tell that Mitsutsuka was now holding his umbrella over both of us. I could smell his scent mixed with the rain, as I stood there nodding repeatedly, like an idiot, unable to take a step. Mitsutsuka didn't move either. He just held the umbrella over me.

We stood there silently in the light rain for a good amount of time. In front of me I saw the buttons of Mitsutsuka's shirt. Cars drove down the lane of traffic just beside us, the red light over his shoulder blurring in the rain. Mitsutsuka suggested in a gentle voice that we have something warm to drink. I nodded and followed him into the cafe.

Sitting across from Mitsutsuka at our usual table, I pulled a small towel out of my bag and offered it to him. Rain dampened his left shoulder, which had gotten wet when he held his umbrella over me. Mitsutsuka said that he was fine, that I was the one who was drenched. He wiped the palms of his hands with his oshibori, then dabbed at his shoulder.

Neither of us said a word; we were as silent as we'd been when we were standing outside in the rain. Our coffee arrived. "This is nice," we both said, then brought the cups to our lips, sipping quietly. In all the countless times that we'd sat here, having coffee or tea, this was the first time we had called the experience "nice."

"This really is nice. I guess we've never said that before," I said after a pause.

"Really?"

"Yeah."

"No kidding."

At the bottom of my bag, I heard my phone ringing. I pulled it out and looked at the screen. It was Hijiri. I snapped the phone shut and dropped it back into my bag. I could hear the muffled ringtone, playing on and on, until it finally stopped.

"Hey," Mitsutsuka said. "Something about you feels different today."

"Oh?" I said, looking down.

"Did you go out somewhere before this?"

"Yeah."

"You did?"

"Yeah."

I looked down at the beads across my chest, catching the light.

"I like your outfit."

"You do?"

"Yeah."

This brought about another stretch of silence. There were no other customers in the cafe, but I could hear someone sneezing loudly in the back. At almost the same moment, I heard a foaming sound outside, like something spilling everywhere at once. I looked out the window to find that what had been a misty fog moments earlier was now a downpour, countless streaks of white beating against the asphalt.

"It's really coming down," I said, watching the rain splash off the sidewalk.

"It's supposed to rain all night."

"I didn't realize," I said.

"That's what they said on TV."

"Mitsutsuka."

"Yes?"

"Do you like talking with me?"

Mitsutsuka shifted in his seat.

"I always like talking with you," he said in a cheerful voice.

"What do you like about it?" I asked.

"What do I like?" He sounded a little baffled. "What do I like about it? That's a tough one." He took a sip of coffee, giving it a second. "I'm sorry, but I don't think I can answer that one on the spot."

"Are there ever times when you don't like it?"

"No, never," Mitsutsuka said. "It's always nice to talk to you."

"Yeah," I said, ". . . but I drink all the time . . . I'm always drinking . . . If I don't drink, and drink a lot, I can't even speak normally. But I haven't had anything to drink today . . . All the times that you met me here and talked with me over the past few months, I was, you know . . ." At this point, I lost my words, unable to say any more.

"Yeah," Mitsutsuka said after a pause. "I know."

The instant I heard this, my cheeks began to burn from the outside, and without meaning to, I looked up at Mitsutsuka.

". . . Of course you noticed. I knew you did."

"Yeah."

"You probably smelled it on me, too."

"I couldn't smell it."

". . . Why didn't you say anything?" I asked. "You don't think it's weird to spend time with a drunk like that? Why didn't you . . . say anything?"

Mitsutsuka paused.

"Everybody has their own reasons."

He tentatively pressed his finger to the scar beside his eyelid, then rubbed at the skin for a long time. I said nothing, looking at his face. The rain was getting even louder. Occasionally the sky would boom with thunder and glow faintly with lightning. The owner of the shop appeared from out back. "Where's it all going to go?" he asked as if talking to himself, then walked past our table and brought his face right up against the glass door to get a good view of the street.

". . . No matter who you are when you come here, Fuyuko, I really do enjoy your company."

But I—I tried to respond, but I was unable to continue.

The steadily mounting sound of rain gathered in my lungs, drowning out the buzzing in my throat before the words could come. Spitting bubbles as I started to sink, I reached for my bag, pulled it over my shoulder, and stood up quietly. I had no idea what I was doing. I had no idea what I wanted. Without looking at Mitsutsuka, I bowed and left the table, heading for the door. Eight steps was all it took. As soon as I was outside, in a storm of such proportions that my imagination failed to grasp where in this gateway to the night the sound was coming from, my body lost its outline and I was unable to open my eyes. Rain streamed from the bottom of my bag, from the ends of my hair, from my elbows and my jaw, puddling in my sneakers as I walked on and on in a succession of steps that felt like they would never end. Just before I went around the corner, I shut my eyes as tightly as I could and breathed out. Then I counted to five, almost praying, then slowly turned around, but there was no one there.

10

I started spending the better half of every day in bed.
When I was working, I managed to focus on the words before me, but only for so long. I called Hijiri to ask if she wouldn't mind scaling back my workload, telling her I wasn't feeling well. That's fine, she said, but what's going on? What's the problem? I said it was nothing, just a migraine I couldn't shake. That the doctor was stumped. All I needed was to cut things back a little—just for the next couple of months. Sure, she said. Of course. Sounds like stress. Get some rest and let me know if I can help. I'll ask my migraine friends for tips, she said. The next week, Hijiri sent me a project that required hardly any research, something I could do without much hassle.

After struggling to focus for two hours at my desk, I would completely lose my drive and climb back under the covers, spending the remainder of the day in a haze. The world passed by without a sound, and the little part of the sky that I could see outside my window moved through a cycle of colors. As I idly stared into the blue of twilight, always coming as a mystery, I gradually lost the ability to tell it from its counterpart at dawn, until I wasn't even able to discern what part of the day it was.

From where I lay in bed, I opened my eyes and saw the spine of the book that Mitsutsuka had given me. Reaching out, I traced the title with a fingertip. Then I picked it up and flipped through the pages. My heart ached as I realized that at some point Mitsutsuka had read over the very same words, or flipped through the pages in the same way. I put down the book and closed my eyes. The melody of the lullaby played on its own in my head, glowing behind my eyelids. I shook my head in an attempt to snap out of it, sighing again and again. After meeting Mitsutsuka that day in the rain, I had stopped listening to the lullaby entirely. I'd also quit drinking.

When I felt sleepy I slept, and when I opened my eyes I got up, letting hunger dictate when to head to the fridge or kitchen cabinet to eat some of the things that I'd stocked up on. When supplies ran out, I started stepping out to the convenience store to grab some snacks, the sort of junk food where it didn't matter if you ate it or not. Even so, I continued to put this food that didn't matter into my body that didn't matter, which made everything seem to matter even less. Every meal, if you could call it a meal, was like another dent in my existence. I couldn't summon the energy to prepare the easiest of foods, exhausted by even the simple act of boiling water.

When lying in bed started to bother me, I got up without actually getting dressed and sat down in my chair, gazing out the window as I wondered what had brought about this awful state of mind. Why did I have to feel so awful all the time? How had I let things get so bad that I was unable to do work or anything else? What was going on? Was it because I wasn't seeing Mitsutsuka? I felt like that had to be part of it. But I also knew that if I really wanted to see him, all I had to do was get on the train on a Thursday or a Sunday, go to the cafe, and I would find him there. I knew he would be kind to me, no different from the way he always was, not upset or anything about how rude I'd been the last time I'd seen him. But I couldn't see him, because seeing him was painful. Meeting up like that was too painful for me. Why was it so painful to meet up with him like that? Because—and then the words failed to come. All I could do was sigh.

I liked Mitsutsuka. I think I liked him from the first time I saw him. But putting it into words made me feel so awful I was unable to sit up in my chair and had to put my head down on my desk. Burrowing my face into my arms, I closed my eyes and said it in a quiet voice. "I like Mitsutsuka." My faltering, raspy voice hung for a moment in my ears before it disappeared entirely. I got up, fell face-down on the bed, and pressed my face into the pillow, letting all the air out of my lungs. Then I lifted my head, flipped over onto my back and tried saying it again. "I like Mitsutsuka." Blood pulsated in my ears; my palms ached, and my throat felt like it could split open any second. Something like nausea welled up from deep inside and I had to squeeze my eyes shut, almost praying for the feeling to subside.

Maybe I wanted Mitsutsuka to hear these words, to know the way I felt. Maybe I wanted him to know, but I wasn't able to tell him, able to say it, able to make my feelings known, and that was why I felt so awful. But if I found a way to tell him how I felt, what exactly would I be telling him? "I like you, Mitsutsuka. I like you." And? What came next? What could possibly happen between the two of us? If I told him that I liked him, I bet Mitsutsuka would nod the way he always did and smile. We'd keep meeting up at the cafe, the same as usual, and he would tell me things, same as usual. But then what? These feelings, these awful feelings, what would happen to them?

Hijiri called me several times, worried about how I was doing, but I lacked the confidence to speak well, so I never answered. At first, she left voicemails, but after leaving ten or so, she gave up. Over time, she called me less and less.

It had been almost three weeks since I had stopped seeing Mitsutsuka.

October was coming to an end, and on my trips to and from the convenience store, I felt the autumn air grow heavier and cooler by the day.

Nothing came from Mitsutsuka. Not a call, not an email, nothing. Not like I was expecting anything, but having a phone that never rang and an inbox without any messages was difficult to bear. When my phone died, I didn't even bother charging it. I just put it in a drawer.

Hijiri sent me several cheery emails, saying she was worried and she wanted to hear from me. I let them go, unable to respond, but after maybe four or five I apologized for never getting to the phone in time and making her worry. I told her that the migraine had yet to let up, and that I knew it was a lot to ask, but I was hoping I could keep on working at this pace for a while. I added that my cell phone battery couldn't seem to hold a charge, but she could reach me by email if anything urgent came up.

The cardboard box that Hijiri had sent me sat open in the corner of my room, which I'd neglected to vacuum for far too long. I'd looked inside the box the second it arrived and pulled out the gray cardigan, which she had packed on top, but I hadn't so much as touched the rest.

I climbed out of bed, sat down with my thighs against the chilly floor, and went through the contents of the box, fanning them out around me. The box was stuffed with clothes that Hijiri had decided she no longer wanted, most of them wrapped in thin, clear plastic from the dry cleaner, stapled with yellow tags stating that they had been cleaned.

I didn't know anything about fashion, but I could tell that each and every garment in the box was top-of-the-line. Examining the tags, I found that there were several brands that even I had heard of, while the designs and textures made it readily apparent that these clothes were entirely unlike anything I owned.

There were cute, crisply ironed shirts with little collars, neatly stacked atop skirts in vivid colors and strange shapes. The three sweaters in the box were all cashmere. There was also a soft jacket made from towel fabric, a dark blue dress knitted from a rough-textured material, and a black cardigan, none of which appeared to have been worn.

Toward the bottom was a camel-colored angora coat, into which a black scarf had been neatly tucked. There was a box under the coat, and I opened it to find two pairs of heels. I remembered how at some point we'd talked about having the same shoe size. Next to the coat was a brown pouch made from silky fabric, bunched up in a ball. I untied the strings and looked inside. It was a two-piece lingerie set, top and bottom. New, with tags.

I stared blankly at Hijiri's clothing, spread across the floor.

After a while, I stood up and grabbed an armful of empty hangers off the adjustable rod that I'd set up in my bedding closet as a makeshift clothing rack and started hanging everything up, one item at a time, but the skinny wire hangers were too flimsy, and I was clearly going to run out. I removed an armload of my old clothes and used those hangers to hang the new clothes from Hijiri.

Now that Hijiri's clothes were occupying most of the rack, my other clothes looked old and faded by comparison. In all likelihood they actually were faded, since they were just a bunch of cheap clothes I'd been wearing long enough that I no longer remembered buying them. They were depressing to look at. Yes, there were shirts, and there were skirts, but my clothes and Hijiri's were so fundamentally different I couldn't believe they could be described using the same words.

I took off my t-shirt and my underwear and walked over to the mirror by the door, then walked back to my room and took the lingerie Hijiri had sent me out of their pouch. Grabbing a fluffy red sweater, wool knee-length skirt, and a pair of heels, I went back to the mirror, where I looked at myself naked, hugging all the clothes. My body was depressing, even worse than my clothes, and I almost shook my head and walked away. I slipped my arms through the straps of Hijiri's bra, noticing the frilly trim, put on the matching underwear and fluffy sweater, zipped up the skirt, stepped into the heels, and stood up straight and tall. This was the first time in my life that I'd worn a skirt that felt so soft against my skin, or worn a red sweater, or worn a pair of heels this high.

I went back into my room and tried on the camel coat. It was so light, nothing like any coat that I'd ever worn. When I slipped a hand into one of the pockets, my fingers found a card for a restaurant called Ne Laissez Pas. I put the card into a drawer and went over to the dresser opposite my closet and rifled through it, pulling out the sweatshirts that I hadn't worn in years, the jeans, the hoodies, the wrinkled, threadbare t-shirts and the rest, gathering them into a ball that I dropped right into the empty cardboard box. At the back of the dresser, I found pants and shirts that I'd bought in my teens, folded flat, and even my gym clothes from middle school, which I had saved, telling myself I could wear them around the house, maybe as pajamas. My nose filled with the smell of clothes that had gone unworn for ages, tinged with the textures of formless memories and landscapes. I even found the sweater that Noriko had given me in high school. I spread it across my lap and spent a moment looking at the cat patch by the hem before tossing it into the box. Whatever of Hijiri's clothes I wasn't able to hang up, I folded carefully and put inside the dresser. When I was finally done, my body felt heavier and heavier, as if the room itself had started to sink without a sound, taking me down with it. Dressed in Hijiri's clothes, I climbed back into bed.

November came and went, one day at a time, without my speaking to anyone. Occasionally a wind from the depths of autumn hit my window with a dry rattle. I spent a few hours of the day with galleys, flipping through reference materials or visiting the library if necessary. Nobody attempted to talk to me, and I made no attempt to talk to anybody else. When I handed the librarian my card or a book, it was like I wasn't even there for her to see. As if I didn't exist anywhere at all.

I started sleeping for hours and hours, having all kinds of dreams throughout the night. Most of these were like layers of images that slipped away once I was awake, but there were other times when I would dream about Mitsutsuka.

The dream was always the same. I'm sitting across from Mitsutsuka, at our table in the cafe, talking the same as always. Without the slightest hesitation, I'm saying things that I could never say to him in real life, acting upset over little things, or saying things that I knew would get under his skin, refusing to forgive him until he made things up to me, just joking around and laughing. We're expressing the way we feel about each other, as if we're lovers, just enjoying our time together. And I always draw Mitsutsuka the same picture: a little house. Running his ballpoint pen over a fresh sheet of paper, I say I want to live with you in a house like this. There's nothing remotely special about the house. It's just a little square affair, the kind you find all over, and yet I improve upon it by adding windows and a door, excitedly explaining how we have to have a certain kind of curtain here, and the roof has to be like this, and we'll put a planter of iceberg roses by the door.

Mitsutsuka tells me it sounds great and sips his coffee, then says it again. It sounds great. Then I tell him that we won't sleep in a bed, we'll have a futon! And it's a little futon, I explain over and over, so we'll have to snuggle up. Mitsutsuka says that sounds great, then nods and asks me where the house is going to be. But as soon as he asks, I get sad. I can't offer a real answer. I say it doesn't matter where, come on, it's time to go to sleep, let's get under the covers and snuggle. Then I grab him by the arm and pull him down.

This is when Mitsutsuka and I get into our little white

futon, snuggling up together, like we do this every night. My head spins with a pleasure so intense it feels like I can barely hold it all inside, amazed that skin pressing against skin could feel this way, at how absorbing body heat—not with the fingers but with the full breadth of the belly or the back—can make it feel as if you're sharing everything there is to share, and every time Mitsutsuka touches me, it sends a new wave crashing through the warm liquid that our bodies are immersed in, so that more than once I feel as if I'm drifting out of consciousness. Overcome by how refreshing and soothing it can be to stare into the eyes of somebody you feel this way about, to be this close to them, as if you're being remade from the deepest parts of you, I bring my open palms to Mitsutsuka's back, nearly trembling at what's happening inside of me, and stroke the same place over and over. But then it hits me that the person lying naked under the futon with Mitsutsuka in her arms isn't actually me, but Hijiri, and as I watch Mitsutsuka's hands stroking the smoothness of her hips, I realize that all of the pleasure that I had just felt wasn't mine at all, but hers. Unsure of where I am, all I can see now is Hijiri's face, so lustrous I can't bring myself to look away, while all that I can hear is Mitsutsuka sighing, a painful moan like he's fighting something. Hijiri's breath envelops him, bringing him gently down into a slickness from which he has no hope of reemerging, as she dampens everything in sight.

One morning after a dream like this, I lay in bed, blinking at the world before my eyes. No matter how I stared, nothing moved, as if a membrane had been stretched over the room. There was no sound, no smell. Passing back and forth over the edge of a fragile sleep, I slipped my hand inside my t-shirt, the way I always did after a dream like this, trying to caress my breasts the way I'd felt Mitsutsuka touch me only moments earlier, to give substance to the feeling. I gently pinched my nipples with my fingertips. I let the hand that had been resting on my belly slip down even further, adding pressure as it went, and pressed into the softness between my legs. But I had no idea what to do next. I had no idea what I could do to return to the place where I'd been only a minute earlier, what it would take to make me feel what I had been feeling again.

I was losing touch with the sensations of the dream every second, as the contours of the things that I could see around me became more and more defined, bringing the quiet recognition that I'd been dreaming all along. I was only dreaming, in my actual apartment, where I actually lived, passing my life in this inconsequential place, my one and only world. My life is nowhere but here, and I am nowhere else. Everything I told Mitsutsuka about snuggling up under the covers and holding each other close had been a dream, bounded by the dream-world, where everything began and ended. The place that I had just been sharing with Mitsutsuka was a dream, nowhere in this world. No matter where or how I looked, I knew that I would never find the time that we had spent together.

Soon whatever had been left of Mitsutsuka disappeared entirely, and when I tried to think about the Mitsutsuka I'd known, it hit me yet again that I knew basically nothing about him. I had no idea what he usually ate, how he spent his time or whom he spent it with, what he cared about, what he thought about throughout the day, where he slept, or where he read. What kind of people he talked to, what they said to make him laugh. What things made him angry or depressed, or what he thought about as he was falling asleep. What kind of women did he like? What kind of women had he fallen for in the past, and how? If I were pretty, would he do the things to the real me that he did when I was dreaming? What were his dreams like? He told me that he liked talking to me, but what if he just likes talking? What made Mitsutsuka sad? What made him happy? What were his dreams? Where was he at this very moment? What was he thinking? What was he doing? Was he fine, maybe even happy not seeing me? Could he take any time, even a second, to think about me?

Face down on the mattress, I pulled the covers over my head and squeezed my eyes shut, waiting for the things swirling in my throat to pass, the breath dampening my cheeks and eyelids endlessly hot and painful.

Midway through November, the sun retreated far into the sky during the day, and the wind was potent with a smell that signaled the coming winter. One afternoon, while I was carrying a finished manuscript to the convenience store fifteen minutes from my house to ship it via parcel service, I saw an accident.

The second that I turned the corner onto the main street, a sound both metallic and explosive, unlike anything I'd ever heard, went off ahead of me, and I instinctively backed up against the nearest building. It took some time for me to understand what had happened, but just as I realized I'd been spared from the event, I saw the body of a man in the road, about ten feet away.

The road was silent, as if the flow of time had been disrupted and brought to a halt. A few other pedestrians were frozen in place, quietly watching the man lying in the road. I have no idea how long we stood there, but the sound of cars running down the opposite lane of traffic broke through the tension in the air and we came together, without anyone taking the lead, looking at one another for an indication of what to do.

"You should call an ambulance," a middle-aged woman said to me. She was wearing a black sun visor.

"Um, I don't have my phone." I swallowed my saliva, barely able to get the words out. A girl with really long hair came from the opposite direction, saying with some excitement in her voice that there'd been an accident, and there was a bike in the middle of the road down the way. I nodded several times and told her I'd heard the noise, it was really loud, then I saw a guy in a suit walking over to us while talking on his phone, explaining in a calm voice where we were and what had happened.

"I called the police," he said. "An ambulance is on the way."

The three of us said just enough to show that we had heard him, nodding at his choice of words but otherwise stock still, standing close enough that we could have touched each other, but all of our eyes were on the man in the street.

He was wearing gray work clothes. There was some kind of writing, maybe a logo, printed on his back, but it was hard to make out what it said. The man's arms and legs were outstretched; he was doubled over, lying in the road, but he looked less like a human being than a piece of cargo that had fallen off a truck. I spotted a shoe that must have come off when he crashed. I also saw his helmet. A good distance beyond him, I saw a black motorized bicycle on its side. Not a single car or motorcycle went by. Drivers coming down the opposing lane slowed down to get a good look, then continued on their way as if nothing had happened.

The man looked like an inanimate object. He didn't so much as twitch; at least from where we stood, I couldn't see even a drop of blood. He looked like a sack dropped on the ashen asphalt. He had a head covered with hair, a torso, two arms and two legs, and he was wearing clothes—a human being no matter how I looked at him, but the longer I stared, the harder it became to see him as a person.

"I don't see any blood," the younger woman said anxiously, pressing her fingers to her lips. She looked up and down the street. "Shouldn't the ambulance be here by now?"

"It'll take a little time," the man said.

"Did he get hit?" the woman in the sun visor asked. Her voice was quiet, like she was speaking to herself. "Did anybody see what happened?"

"I heard it, and when I looked up, he was like this," I said, then noticed two dark black streaks in the road, unsure if they had been left by the braking tires or the body of the motorized bicycle.

I suspect that each of us was wondering whether the man was alive or dead, but no one even hinted at the question. Holding the envelope with the manuscript in both hands, I heard my pulse thumping in my ears. Was he dead? Or had he simply lost consciousness? I had no idea. How can it be so hard to tell? We stared at the man's body from afar, as if it were a hunk of clay, or an abandoned glove, not one of us stepping off of the sidewalk and into the street to take a closer look.

Ambulance and police sirens wailed around the corner, screaming as they pulled up in a crash of sounds that drowned the sounds made by our eyes and mouths. More people were stopping now, wanting to find out what had happened, a crowd of strangers forming almost out of nowhere.

Clutching the manuscript against my chest, I distanced myself from the crowd and took a series of deep breaths. I saw the man in the suit who had made the call talking with one of the police officers. The other officer was taking notes, sometimes touching a finger to his ear and saying something over the radio. The younger woman and the woman with the sun visor were nowhere in sight.

It seemed like it had been a long time since they had arrived, but I watched as they finally loaded the man into the ambulance and drove away. Once they were gone, I walked to the convenience store, where I handed the envelope to the clerk and paid the fee.

Back home, I carefully washed my hands with soap, did the

same to my face, then sat down on the floor and watched the day transition into night. As the dresser and the floor and the walls and the places where they met sank into blue, I stared at my hands, my skin, and the outline of my body taking on the same blue as every other object in the room. I flipped my hands over occasionally, made a fist or spread my fingers. There were so many wrinkles, so many joints in my fingers, veins bulging from the backs of my hands.

Sitting at my desk, I took the CD player out of the drawer, put the earphones in my ears, and pressed play. The CD Mitsutsuka gave me was still inside, and I watched it start to spin. But before the first note, I pressed stop, pulled out the earphones, balled up the cord, and put it on my desk. In the same drawer, I found my dead cell phone and placed it in the middle of my desk, keeping both hands on it as I gave it a long look. I flipped it open, then flipped it shut. Then I flipped it open one more time and ran my fingertip across the black screen repeatedly. It left a streaky fingerprint. I didn't move for some time. Then a question suddenly came to me. What had I been doing up until now?

Had I ever chosen anything? Had I made some kind of choice that led me here? Thinking it over, I stared at the cell phone in my hands. The job that I was doing, the place where I was living, the fact that I was all alone and had no one to talk to. Could these have been the result of some decision that I'd made?

I heard a crow crying somewhere in the distance and turned to the window. It occurred to me that maybe I was where I was today because I hadn't chosen anything.

I applied to whatever colleges my teacher suggested and fell into a job after graduation, which I'd left only because I had to escape. I was only able to go freelance because of all the legwork that Hijiri did for me. Had I ever chosen anything on my own, made something happen? Not once. And that's why I was here now, all alone.

But I asked myself: Haven't you always done your best with whatever you were up against? Haven't you given it your all, whatever came your way? Unfortunately, no. That's not how things had been for me. I had faked it the whole way. In all those years of doing whatever I was told to do, I had convinced myself that I was doing something consequential, in order to make excuses for myself, as I was doing right now, and perpetually dismissed the fact that I'd done nothing with my life, glossing over it all. I was so scared of being hurt that I'd done nothing. I was so scared of failing, of being hurt, that I chose nothing. I did nothing.

My thoughts turned to Mitsutsuka.

I thought about the culture center where we'd met, and how alone I'd felt until the day I met him. How when I lost my bag, Mitsutsuka kept me company, even going with me to the police. I thought about the coffee. And the thousand yen I borrowed. About how we walked back to the station on that brilliant day, the way he turned by the stairs and came back. About the first time that he said my name. His voice, the way he said it. The faded patches of his worn-out dark blue polo shirt. The fraying corners of his shoulder bag. How his shoulders and his back turned slightly inward. All about light. The things he'd taught me, going slow to make sure I understood. About the lullaby with a melody made of light. About the pens in his chest pocket. I could remember all the separate things that I had seen him do or heard him say, and yet I was unable to remember the substance of our conversations, or how we'd passed the time.

I had to see him. The thought made my heart jump. I had to see Mitsutsuka or I would lose the only thing that really mattered. My only treasures were the memories of how it felt when we met up and talked, but they were disappearing, and soon they'd be gone forever. Truly lost. I ran the risk of losing the one thing that really mattered to me. The way he talked, and the way he walked, all the things that had accumulated over the few months we'd spent together.

The next thing I knew, the sun had set, leaving the room completely dark. If I focused, I could just barely see the hands of the clock pointing to five-thirty. I found the cell-phone charger in my drawer and plugged the phone into an outlet in the kitchen, then held the power button down. The phone made a sound as it came to life. The screen was so bright that it made me squint, and I sat down on the kitchen floor in the dark for what felt like forever.

I pressed a button to open up my address book and scrolled to Mitsutsuka. *Mitsutsuka*. His name appeared in the light. Holding the phone in my left hand, I closed my eyes, then slowly opened them again. I pressed call. After a couple of seconds, it started to ring, so loudly that my breath caught up with my pulse. I bent forward as far as I could go, and held the phone against my ear.

"Hello?" I heard Mitsutsuka say.

I was unable to respond. Hello? I heard him say again.

"Hello," I said, except my voice was so hoarse I was worried that he couldn't even hear me, so I said hello a second time.

"Hello?" he asked.

"It's Irie."

"Hello . . . ?"

"It's me, Irie. Can you hear me?"

"Fuyuko," Mitsutsuka said, using my first name.

"Mitsutsuka," I said his name quietly. My palms were throbbing. "How have you been?"

"Fine, fine. How about you?"

"Oh, I've been good."

"Glad to hear it. It feels like it's been a while," Mitsutsuka said.

"Yeah, it does," I said back.

Both of us went silent, but a few moments later, I heard Mitsutsuka let out a small cough. "What have you been up to?" Mitsutsuka asked.

"Just working at home," I said. "What about you, Mitsutsuka?"

"Me? I've been working, too."

"Really?"

"Yeah."

Then came another block of silence.

"By the way," Mitsutsuka said. "I've been listening to nothing but Chopin for the last month or so."

"Really?"

"And I caught a cold, a pretty bad one. It lasted a while, too. I must be getting old."

"So you haven't been fine after all, have you?"

"Now that you mention it, no, I guess I haven't," he said and laughed.

"But you're feeling better now?"

"Yeah, I think so," he said. As if he'd just remembered, he added that the year was almost over.

"You sound a little like a teacher," I said, cracking up a bit.

"Probably because I am."

"Fair enough."

"Some places have already put up their Christmas lights," he said.

"It's about that time of year."

"They probably put them up at night, don't they?"

"Yeah, probably."

This was the first time in a long time I'd heard his voice, but Mitsutsuka sounded exactly the same. He spoke as if we had been talking at the cafe only yesterday, picking up right where we'd left off.

Experiencing a strange emotion that I couldn't understand, like sadness and relief mixed with bitterness and something close to anger, I felt my body being chipped away, getting smaller by the second. After a month and a half, I was finally hearing Mitsutsuka's voice. There I was, in the very moment I had been waiting for. How badly had I wanted to meet him over the past month and a half? How often had I thought about him? My heart was bursting with these reawakened feelings, and before I knew it I was no longer able to speak.

" . . . Well, I'm going to hang up now," I said eventually.

"Okay," Mitsutsuka said.

Kneeling on the pitch-black kitchen floor, I hung my head and sat completely still, the phone between my shoulder and my ear slick with sweat and exhalation. The compressor of the fridge was humming. I was beginning to doubt whether Mitsutsuka was still there, on the other end of the line. Maybe he'd already hung up. I closed my eyes in the darkness, gripped the phone and asked him something in a small voice.

"Mitsutsuka, are you married?"

No, he said after a moment. With my eyes closed, I took a deep breath, letting the air fill my chest and held it there before letting it all out.

"Have you ever thought about sleeping with me?"

I could tell that Mitsutsuka was still there. Eyes closed, I listened to my pulse in my ears and counted the beats. Mitsutsuka said nothing. I couldn't tell if he'd missed what I had said, or if he simply wanted to pretend as though he had. Either way, I had to ask again. I had to. The fingertips of my right hand were trembling.

Have you ever thought about sleeping with me?

Yes, he said.

I looked up into the darkness.

You have, I said, practically talking to myself.

I have, he said quietly.

So have I, for a long time now, I said, squeezing the words out. After saying them, I felt like I was going to collapse. With my hand pressed against my buzzing throat, I fell down on the kitchen floor.

From there, I have no idea what we said, or how the conversation ended. It was like I was tracing another person's dream with my finger. I know there were many more moments of silence, and that Mitsutsuka laughed a little, and I sort of laughed too. We made plans to meet up two weeks later, on the tenth of December, Mitsutsuka's birthday. Talking with Mitsutsuka, I felt as if I was back inside the dream that I'd had so many times over the past month and a half. After we hung up, I spent a few minutes in the warm darkness, leaning against the kitchen wall. Stuck in a gentle fog, I steadied my head and managed to stand up and stagger over to the bed, where I let everything go all at once, and fell flat on the mattress. A dizzying, quiet excitement spread to every corner of the room and swallowed me whole. For a while, I was unable to move. At some point, after who knows how long, I pulled back the covers and slipped my arms and legs inside, warm against the coolness of the sheets. I rested one hand on my thigh and brought the fingers of the other to my neck. Blood was coursing through me, heating my body. Then I took both hands and held my phone to my chest, squeezing it as hard as I could, replaying in my head everything that Mitsutsuka had just said to me, hundreds of times, then shut my eyes.

11

With every motion, a fragrant air escaped the fabric of Mitsutsuka's coat, although it took some time for me to realize that it was the smell of winter.

"It's winter," I said.

"It sure is," Mitsutsuka said. The hilly street that led down from Shinagawa Station to the restaurant was lined with trees strung with Christmas lights, and we stopped from time to time to look at them.

"Almost everyone's switched over to those blue lights," Mitsutsuka said, "but I'm a fan of these old-fashioned ones."

"The yellow ones feel warmer, don't they?"

"And the bulbs are built to last. They don't make them like they used to."

"The bluer ones feel so cold."

Finding Mitsutsuka at the station, after two months without seeing his face, I bowed and had to turn away, unable to look right at him. Here it is, I said, pointing at the map that I had printed out at home. Without making eye contact, we looked over the route, then explored a handful of vanilla topics as we walked side by side down the street where night had fallen. What sort of books have you been working on? I'm proofreading a collection of essays and interviews. Oh yeah? Yeah. How's school? Just a few more weeks until winter break. But we've still got makeup exams. You do? Yeah. We walked along one step at a time, as if the soles of our feet were marking the silences in our disjointed conversation. This was basically the first time in my life I'd worn heels, and I had no idea how to walk in them without hurting my feet, but I was in a cheerful mood as I walked beside Mitsutsuka. I was wearing the matching set of underwear along with a thin green cashmere sweater, a dark blue skirt made of soft wool, and the camel coat. A stranger to perfume, I had to read an article online about where to apply it; whenever I moved, I caught a whiff of fragrance rising from my hips.

The restaurant was in a large, renovated house in a residential area. When I opened the massive wooden door, a woman with long hair in a long black dress came up to welcome us with a bow. In a quiet voice, she asked for my name. I told her Irie, and she gave us both a winning smile. We've been expecting you, please come in, she said, then led us swiftly down the hall.

Under the tall ceiling, a dozen or so tables had been generously spaced throughout the restaurant, where couples were drinking wine. Several different chandeliers were hanging throughout the room, their countless glass teardrops shimmering with every color of the rainbow. Ceramic curiosities with minute designs lined antique shelves while brightly colored abstract art added a tasteful contrast. The wooden floors had been polished to a sheen. As we followed the woman to our table, I watched my step to make sure my heels didn't land between the boards.

Opening a skinny yellow door at the back, she led us into a private room, with candles flickering everywhere. It took my breath away. A trio of brass candlesticks sat on the white cloth spread across our table, while the shelves arranged symmetrically along the walls were stocked with all kinds of candles—fat ones and tall ones, white, pale yellow and blue ones—each of them burning with a little orange flame that fluttered as if whispering.

I was shown to the far seat, and Mitsutsuka took the seat

across from me. The woman came back carrying a black leather-bound menu. I'd requested the full-course dinner for two when I made the reservation, so I asked her in a low voice if we could have what I had asked for on the phone. She smiled, assuring me that everything was taken care of, and asked what we would like to drink. At the news that drinks were not included with the meal, I felt a heat behind my ears. I stared for some time at the words and prices of the drink list, no idea what to order, but then she pointed at a wine and said that it would pair nicely with our meal. I didn't know if it was expensive for a bottle of wine, but when I glanced at the prices for the other bottles and found that it was the cheapest option, I nodded and asked her for that one. I'll be right back, she said, and left the room.

Mitsutsuka and I both sat with our hands resting in our laps, looking here and there around the room, eventually taking quiet sips from the glasses of water in front of us before looking once more at the candles along the walls. It's so pretty, I said. Mitsutsuka nodded and agreed. It sure is. But once I said that it was pretty, I felt like there was nothing left to say and turned to watch the wobbling flames. There was a knock, and the woman entered carrying our wine. She placed large glasses by our fingertips. We watched her lift the bottle with a practiced hand and pour us each a glass.

"Happy birthday," I said in a quiet voice, a moment after the woman had left the room.

"It's not my real birthday yet," Mitsutsuka laughed. "Yours is coming up soon, too. Maybe we should have planned this as a celebration for both of us."

"No, today we're celebrating you," I said, laughing. The fact that Mitsutsuka had remembered my birthday made me so happy that I almost felt like I might really smile for once.

"Today was the only day they had an opening. I wish we could have made it for your actual birthday."

"No," Mitsutsuka said, giving the room another look. "This is great."

"Anyway, happy birthday," I said and bowed.

"What's better than a pre-birthday?"

"Pre-birthday?" I asked.

"Right, because we're celebrating in advance," he said.

"Is that a thing? I had no idea," I said, deeply impressed.

"No, I guess people don't say that. It's just something I made up." Mitsutsuka sounded a little nervous as he spoke. He wiped his forehead with his palm. I saw that he was sweating faintly.

"Well, happy . . . pre-birthday," I said, laughing a little as I raised my glass a couple inches off the table.

"This is the best pre-birthday I can remember," Mitsutsuka said. We clinked glasses and the sound rang through the air. Our eyes met for a fraction of a second before both of us looked away and drank our wine in silence.

Each time the woman brought over an expertly plated clam sauté or surimi salad, she gave us precise explanations of the way the dish was cooked and the provenance of its ingredients, but since it took every ounce of effort I possessed just to answer her and nod at the food, I retained basically nothing.

"I've never eaten one of these before," Mitsutsuka whispered, biting into one of the olives that had come with the bread.

"What do you think?" I asked.

"I can't really get a read on the flavor," Mitsutsuka said, moving his mouth. "Though I guess flavor is something we make up in our heads, so maybe I just don't know where to put it yet."

"I think this is my second time eating olives."

"Not exactly sour . . . just kind of strange. But I think I've got it now." Mitsutsuka nodded with finality and washed the olives down with wine. Unsure if I was feeling crazy or happy, I hung my head and laughed without making a sound.

This was my first time seeing Mitsutsuka drink alcohol or eat food. Seeing him pick up the bread, rip off a chunk, and put it in his mouth, I had no idea what I should be doing with my eyes. Every time this happened, I would pick up my knife and fork and cut whatever was on my plate.

The wine disappeared in no time, and when the woman came back to retrieve our plates, I ordered another bottle of the same. I came prepared with fifty-thousand yen in my wallet, and told myself there was no way this could cost more than that. Regardless, this was a celebration, and tonight was my treat.

When the woman returned with a fresh set of plates, then left the room again, we sat in utter silence with our hands resting on the tablecloth. The candles threw various shadows on the walls, trembling in spurts. It was just the two of us, alone, surrounded by little flames.

"You look really striking today," Mitsutsuka said a little too quickly as our eyes met. You really think so? I asked, looking down with a hand pressed to my throat.

I'd let my hair grow out for about a year, doing absolutely nothing to take care of it, but that night, before meeting up with Mitsutsuka, I decided I would have it trimmed a bit, and visited a hair salon near the station.

"Just an inch or so," I said.

The beautician, whose hair was styled like a Maltese, sat me down in one of two chairs and gave my hair a thorough brushing before wetting it with a spray bottle.

"You've got beautiful hair," she said, sounding impressed as she combed it. "I almost never see hair so straight and healthy."

No one had ever said something like this to me before. I wasn't sure how to respond, so I just nodded slightly, looking in the mirror.

"Ever had a perm?" the woman asked, lifting a strand of hair to take a close look at the ends.

"No, never."

"Right? I could tell." She pinched a lock of my hair between her fingers and clipped it with the shears.

"You've got a date tonight?" she asked in an eager tone of voice. No, I answered automatically, then wavered before saying, actually, yes. Oh really, she said, sliding behind me in her rolling chair and checking to see how long my hair was. You're young and beautiful, she said with a laugh. Enjoy it.

"You've got great style, too," she said, looking into my eyes through the mirror. "You look like you came right out of a magazine."

"That isn't true." I shook my head.

"But it is. I know good clothes when I see them. And look how thin you are."

"I'm not," I said, shaking my head again.

"Sure you are. Do you have a special place where you get all these clothes?"

"Yeah, I guess I do."

Before long she finished with the scissors, made a quick pass with the hairdryer, then gave me a thorough blowout after which my hair had such a nice shine I thought it almost looked like a wig. When I bobbed my head, the hoops of light followed along, making me feel like I'd made a great discovery. To think my hair could look like this if I only dried it properly. Just looking at it made my face relax into a smile.

"What about makeup?" the woman asked me, examining my face through the mirror. Not a thought in my head, I started stammering and told her yes, uh, after the hair. Great, she said, it's on the house, and since you have a date, I'll make it extra special. She gave my shoulders a tap, went over to a shelf at the back, and returned with a large floral-print makeup case.

"Look at your skin," she said with a sigh. "You practically don't even need foundation."

The best I could do was say thank you. She walked the sponge and her fingers all over my face. Commenting on the coolness of my eyes, she said that blue might do the trick, even if it is winter, and applied a deep blue eyeshadow over my eyelids. With single eyelids like yours, eyeliner on the top lid would be tough, she said. You'd get a sticky mess whenever you blink. Same for me. Alright, let's accentuate these cool eyes of yours with some liner on the bottom lid, she said, drawing a fine eyeliner pencil along the boundary between my eyeball and my bottom eyelid, skirting my eye, then used the same pencil to trace the outline of my eyebrow over and over. Next, she applied a lipstick that had such a strong fragrance it stung my nose, then turned toward the mirror several times to nod at me approvingly. Finally, she puckered her lips, signaling for me to do the same. The lipstick was so thick that my lips practically stuck together. Dab them a bit, the woman said as she handed me a tissue. When I pressed it to my lips, it left a striking pattern in the dark pink on the tissue, like a print made with a fish. The whole process took only a few minutes. A simple makeup job, she said, just the essentials. She gave me a hand mirror, inside of which I found a version of myself that I'd never seen.

"Even prettier with makeup," she said, overjoyed.

"Thank you," I nodded, staring at myself in the mirror, concerned for a moment that the makeup was way too much, but when I looked more closely, my eyebrows and eyes looked bolder, making me look like a strong-willed individual. As I turned my face to see myself from different angles, I realized how different I looked, and set the little mirror down to look at my reflection in the giant mirror on the wall. I felt an emotion bubbling up from deep inside, and if I had to give the feeling a name, it would be giddiness.

"Striking?" I asked Mitsutsuka. The candles in the brownish orange stands on the table flared up suddenly, illuminating Mitsutsuka's left cheek.

"Striking," he said again with a smile. I almost asked him what he meant by striking, but I took a sip of wine to drown out the question.

"There's something else, though. You look a little different from usual," he said, smiling.

"Really?" I asked, smiling back.

"Have you been here before?" Mitsutsuka asked me, almost whispering.

"It's my first time, but a friend said it was good, so I made a reservation."

"It has a funny name, don't you think?" Mitsutsuka said, squinting as he looked around the room. "What was it again? Nu Ray . . ."

"Ne Laissez Pas," I laughed. "It does sound kind of funny."

The wine was nice. Each time we met eyes and looked away, we took another drink. Under the effects of the alcohol, I could feel all of these invisible things that existed between Mitsutsuka and me—air, distance, memories—morphing gracefully into a visceral mass. Both of us had had quite a bit to drink. When the woman came to take away the plates that we'd finished with, I asked her what the name of the restaurant meant.

"It's French," she told us with a grin. "It means 'Don't Leave.'"

Over the sounds of knives and forks scraping against plates, we could hear bursts of laughter from the people seated beyond the door, in the main part of the restaurant. Their laughter made us look at one another. When our eyes met, we sort of smiled and looked down at our plates, or reached for our glasses of wine. Watching each other, we ate pieces of vegetables or took bites of the meat that we'd sliced into thin pieces with our knives, savoring the liquid that oozed out with the whole of our tongues. We chewed and chewed until the pieces lost their shape and we were sure that they couldn't get any softer, then let the food slip gently down our throats.

Your final dish, the woman said, setting down a glossy blue ceramic bowl. We peered inside. It was some kind of brownish soup, devoid of any identifiable ingredients. Please have a taste, she said, gesturing toward the soup. We picked up our new spoons and touched their backs to the surface of our soup. The way they sank revealed the broth to have a silky texture, and if you stirred it with your spoon, round morsels bobbed up from the bottom of the dish. Have a taste, the woman said, and so we did, bringing our spoons to our lips.

"It's soil soup," the woman explained, hands folded at her stomach.

"Soil?" Mitsutsuka asked. I took another look inside the bowl and asked if dirt was edible.

"When properly prepared, it's safe to eat. We boil it for several hours, which kills off any bacteria, then carefully skim off the impurities and pass it through a strainer," she said. "Then we finish it off with gelatin."

After the woman bowed and left, we went back to the soil soup. The clumps rising from the bottom of the bowl were soil. I scooped some up and had a taste. What filled my mouth made a grating sound against my teeth. Mitsutsuka scooped up a bit of soil too. Without a word, we watched each other chewing tentatively. I focused on the flames quivering in Mitsutsuka's eyes.

"Really, I should pay," Mitsutsuka said. We'd stopped around the corner, a few minutes from the restaurant. I shook my head and laughed, reminding him we'd come to celebrate his birthday. Mitsutsuka looked skeptical, but I simply turned ahead and started walking, and a moment later I could hear his footsteps catching up with me.

"That was good wine," I said. It was my first time drinking with Mitsutsuka, and the alcohol was spreading pleasantly throughout my body. As the night went on, my hands and feet became increasingly lighter. My heels made satisfying clicks. I was happy that my coat was so light. I remembered how my face had looked that evening at the salon. How Mitsutsuka complimented me, saying I looked striking. The hoops of light in my hair. I turned around and stopped, looking Mitsutsuka in the eye.

"There's a novel with a girl who eats dirt," he said.

"A novel?" I asked.

"Yeah, a really long one. I forget what it's called. Anyway, the girl eats dirt, lots of it, but hides it from her mother. She knows it's wrong, but she can't stop."

"So why's she do it?" I asked, but Mitsutsuka went quiet, as if something had just occurred to him, and for a moment he stood there. "Mitsutsuka?"

"Sorry," he laughed. "What were you saying?"

"Nothing," I said. "Is everything okay?"

It's fine, he said, laughing a little.

"I guess I just remembered something. Something that I hadn't thought about in a really long time."

I stared at the side of his face.

"It was my dad," he said, speaking in a slightly lower voice.

"Your dad?"

"Well, this was a really long time ago, and it's possible that I'm confusing him with someone else," he said, shaking his head. "My dad never ate dirt . . . This was back in the old days, but he used to eat raw rice all the time, and I'd forgotten all about it, until now."

"Raw rice? Uncooked?"

"Yeah," Mitsutsuka said. "He always had handfuls of rice in his jacket pockets. He'd grab some and slip it into his mouth like it was gum or something. It made my mom so angry. She was always telling him to stop, that it was disgusting. But habits like that can be really hard to break. It's the sort of thing you don't even realize you're doing. My dad taught high school, and from what I hear, he even did it in class. My mom was so ashamed. She hated that he did that. They were always getting into arguments about it. Looking back now, though, it was actually kind of peaceful in its own way."

I nodded a few times, studying Mitsutsuka's face.

"My mom left when I was still in school. For a while it was just me and my dad in the house, until the last few years of his life. I watched him eating raw rice the whole time, but somehow I forgot, like it never even happened." Mitsutsuka laughed. "I guess we can forget pretty much anything . . . I don't know why I'm telling you this. Sorry, what were we talking about?"

"Oh . . . about the girl, in that novel. Why was she eating dirt?" I said the words in a low voice, staring deep into his eyes.

"I don't think we ever find out," Mitsutsuka said. "I forget the details. I'm pretty sure I wouldn't have remembered anything at all, if we hadn't had soil soup tonight."

We took our time walking to the station.

I stretched out my fingers and swung my arms, walking like I was swimming through the air. The Chopin lullaby started playing in my head, and I tried humming the melody. Know what song this is? Sure, it's the lullaby. That's right. You're a pretty good singer, aren't you, Fuyuko? No, I'm hopeless. Really? You sound great to me. Really? Can you sing, Mitsutsuka? I'm as hopeless as they come. Then I guess there's no hope for either of us.

I stared at Mitsutsuka, a couple of steps behind him but off to the side, humming the rest of the lullaby. Hey, Fuyuko, watch your step, Mitsutsuka said, sounding worried as he held out his hand.

A gust of wind blew down the street. The next thing I knew, we were standing under a tree I couldn't name, gazing up into innumerable leaves quaking in unison. Nearby a crow cried out, and the edges of the night were thrown into stark relief. It was just the two of us, in the shadows of the night.

"The wind's really blowing," I said, paddling the air. "And look at the shadows. Have you ever seen shadows like this at night?"

"They're so sharp," Mitsutsuka said. Another gust went by, blowing Mitsutsuka's hair over his ears and across his forehead.

"Hey, Mitsutsuka, is there really nothing here?" I asked, looking him straight in the face.

"Here? Where?"

"Here," I said, pointing my hand at the space between our bodies.

"There's plenty," Mitsutsuka said. "Try waving your hand around. Can't you feel it?"

"Yeah, I guess I can," I said, swinging my hands through the air.

"Right?" Mitsutsuka said, drawing a circle in midair with his finger. "Can't you feel the motion of the air?"

"Yeah," I said.

"You're touching particles."

"Particles . . ." I said to myself.

"That's right. Particles."

For a while, Mitsutsuka and I moved our hands up and down and side to side. He looked so serious that I started cracking up. Mitsutsuka laughed too. Once it was out of our systems, we both fell silent, and another gust of wind went by. In a single shadow, we locked eyes, gazing at one another.

Mitsutsuka, I called his name. Mitsutsuka only looked at me, no response. Without either of us taking the lead, our hands touched. The backs of our fingers were pressed together. We didn't move. The night passing through the trees above us left a faint pattern on his cheeks. Can I touch the light, I asked him in a soft voice, examining its shape. In a way you can, but in another you can't, he answered just as quietly. I could hear his breath as if it was inches from my ear. Mitsutsuka, I said. Can I touch you? I lifted his hand and gave his fingers a squeeze. Are you touching me right now? It's the same as the light, Mitsutsuka said, letting me grip his fingers. Touching can be a difficult state to define. In a way, touching means you can't get any closer. I stared at Mitsutsuka's fingers, held tightly within my own. There he was, and there I was, the same person who was paralyzed by loneliness at home, but here, touching him. The thought of this made my scalp tingle and my chest tighten. I'm touching you, I said quietly. If this means I can't get any closer, I'm fine with that, because I'm touching you. When I looked up, his face was right in front of me. The darks of his eyes were wet, carrying a trace of light. I reached out my other hand and gently touched my fingertips to the scar by his eye. Mitsutsuka, I love you, I'm in love with you. The words came spilling from my heart, far stronger than they had ever sounded at home, without him there, when I'd woken up from a dream, only to watch them break apart. I'm in love with you. No sooner than I said the words, tears formed in my eyes, enough to make it seem as if the space between my eyes and eyelids had expanded. Tears ran down my cheeks onto my chin, where they merged into a stream of drops that fell into the night. I didn't even blink; the tears rushed down my cheeks like animals bound for the night, as if running from something, running from me, in a stream that showed no sign of letting up. Making a complete mess of my face, I cried and cried, for the first time in so long I could barely even find the memory, but knew that when it happened, when that happened, I wished I could have cried this hard, a knowledge that translated into tears, more tears than I could ever hope to stop. But I had to remind myself that I was not in a memory of any kind, but standing here, standing in front of Mitsutsuka, reflected in his eyes, where I could see that I was crying. Mitsutsuka let me squeeze his fingers, not saying anything, standing still for me. This was the first time I learned what it feels like to cry with someone there, watching over you.

Not saying a word, just standing there, Mitsutsuka looked like he was waiting patiently for my tears to settle. I heard a car go by, not very far away from us. Using my palm, I wiped the tears dripping down my chin, then rubbed my eyes, covered my face, and started crying again. Mitsutsuka lifted his free hand and rested it on the crown of my head. I thought I could feel the heat of his hand entering my skin. With his palm still on my head, I asked Mitsutsuka if he would spend my birthday with me, in a voice that was almost all sob. Will you walk through the night with me? And will you listen to that song with me, just the two of us?

The tears were still coming. When his hand moved from my head, I looked up and saw that he was looking at me, nodding over and over. He looked like he was sort of smiling. Seeing him like that, I buried my face in my hands and started crying out loud.

Remembering the texture of a dream I'd once had, I walked back to the station, rode on a crowded train, went through the gates, and found myself outside my local station.

The wind was strong, so I buttoned up my coat. As time went by, the cold that I had not so much as noticed earlier had deepened to a chill, but I was somehow still asleep in that elusive dream, my outstretched body floating in the heat of memory.

I found my CD player in my bag, put my earphones in my ears, and pressed play. After a brief silence, the familiar sound of the piano came alive, and I let out a heavy sigh. The white light of the streetlamps quivered, the windows of the quiet houses reflected the chilly smell of night, and the trees rustled in the wind as if aflame. I waved my arms through the air like I was swimming, like I always did at home. Reveling in the joy that I felt pouring from the melody, I thought about spending my birthday with Mitsutsuka, spending time with Mitsutsuka on that special night. *Mitsutsuka*. When I said his name inside my head, my palms tingled with remembered sensations, my chest aching with happiness. The melody of the piano mixed with the invisible particles around me and turned to wind, stroking my hair and skin as my body opened a path through its softness. Recalling everything that had happened that night in minute detail, I put my hands on my head and softly sang the lullaby. I was almost to my apartment when I saw what looked like a person near the telephone pole by the stairs, trembling in the dark. I stopped, pulled the earphones from my ears, and fixed my eyes on the spot. Focusing, and careful not to move, I saw someone, this time for sure. I braced myself and stepped back, but it seemed like they'd already seen me. A moment later, I saw them step under the streetlight.

It was Hijiri.

12

D id I scare you?"

Hijiri took a few steps toward me. I couldn't believe that anybody was sneaking around out here, much less Hijiri, and for a moment I was speechless. I stepped back automatically, balled up the earphones that were in my hand, and stuffed them in my bag. Hijiri stood in the shadows and looked me in the face.

"I thought you weren't feeling well," she said, "but you look pretty good to me."

"What are you doing here?" I finally managed to ask. "What are you doing?"

"You said you weren't feeling well," Hijiri said. "I came to see how you were holding up."

I switched my tote bag to my other shoulder and stood there for a moment without saying anything. Hijiri looked at me from the pale light of the streetlamp. She was wearing a black coat with a brown fur collar, black tights, and black high heels. For a while, we just stood there staring at each other, neither of us daring to speak. Wind blew down the street again and again, the dry sound of moving branches filling the space between us. I had no desire to move, but I knew we couldn't stand outside forever, so I braced myself and started walking toward the entrance to my building.

"You're not going to ask me how I knew where you lived?" Hijiri asked. Shadows fell on her face. It was black around her eyes, and her face looked a little pale.

"You have my address," I said quietly. This made Hijiri

laugh so hard that she almost doubled over, but then she lost her balance and toppled forward. It was hard to tell from where I stood, but she could have been a little drunk.

"You seem fine to me," Hijiri said. "How's the mystery migraine? All gone?"

"Yeah, a lot better, thanks," I said.

"Hey, have you been drinking?" Hijiri gave me a look that felt like it would never end. "I saw you coming this way, sort of dancing."

"I just had a little," I said.

"Huh. And here I thought you couldn't drink. Something happen?"

I had no idea how to explain myself, so I said nothing.

"You really should have told me you were feeling better," she said coldly. "You know how busy we are right now. I covered for you. The least you could do is tell me what's going on, or what your plans were."

"I'm sorry."

"Is this too hard for you to understand?"

"No," I said, shaking my head. "I understand."

"Then why didn't you say anything?" Hijiri asked.

I was silent, no idea how to respond.

"Anyway, I just wanted to see how you were doing. Hey, it's kind of cold out here. I'm cold. Let me in."

Hijiri folded her arms and shivered.

I looked at her. She looked at me. Then she looked me up and down and said, wait a second, those are my clothes, and sort of laughed without using her voice. You fooled me for a minute, she said. They look totally different on you. Amazing. She shivered again. Come on, I'm cold, she said, shaking all over. Without another word between us, I continued to the entrance and climbed the stairs to my floor. Hijiri followed. Our heels clanged out of sync on the steel stairs.

"Can I sit here?"

Sure, I said. I got myself a bottle of tea from the fridge and brought it into my room. Hijiri sat on the bed and looked around, grinning as she complimented me on keeping things so neat and organized.

I had more or less nothing to say, but I pulled out my desk chair and sat down a safe distance from her, still in my coat, then looked over the label of the bottle of tea that I was holding without exactly reading what it said.

"Hey, are you wearing makeup?" Hijiri asked me, interest piqued. "It was too dark outside to tell. What's going on? Drinking when you never drink, going out with makeup on. Really, though, what's going on with your makeup?" She laughed giddily.

"I had something I had to do today."

"I'm sure you did, but . . . I mean, just look at you. Look at your face. That blue is out of control. And those circles under your eyes. They're literally black. It's even under your nose. Hold on, Fuyuko. You came home like this?" Looking utterly incredulous, Hijiri hugged a pillow to her chest and doubled over laughing. "What the hell happened?"

I listened to her laugh, declining to comment. Then I ran a finger under my eye. It left a black smudge on my fingertip. I rubbed the skin over and over, but the smear on my finger wouldn't go away. I thought about that word again: *striking*.

"So what was this thing you had to do?" Hijiri asked, done laughing for the moment.

"I was meeting somebody," I said. My voice was oddly hoarse. I coughed, but I couldn't clear my throat.

"Who'd you meet?" Hijiri asked me with a smile. I didn't want to answer, so I was silent. Why can't you tell me, she asked. Is it a secret? It's not like that, was all I could say.

"Was it a guy?" Hijiri asked, not letting up. "You met up with a guy, didn't you?"

I didn't answer.

"Come on. Just tell me. I mean, everything you're wearing is mine, top to bottom. I kinda feel like I contributed to this somehow. Besides, it's only fair. When you've asked me about my love life, I've never held back, have I?"

I exhaled through my nose, staring at the bottle of tea.

"I went out to eat. That's all."

"With your boyfriend?"

"No, it's not like that."

"What's it like, then? He's just a friend of yours?"

"Not exactly."

"So what is he?"

I couldn't say anything. I just went silent.

"Don't tell me you're fuck buddies," Hijiri said teasingly and laughed. "What? Am I wrong?"

"Are you drunk?" I asked.

Hijiri fell back on the bed, let out a quick laugh, then sat up again, not giving me an answer.

"I mean, if he's not your boyfriend, and he's not your friend, and you're not fucking him, then who is he?" Hijiri asked, looking genuinely stumped.

After a long pause, I quietly said, "I like him."

"Huh?"

Hijiri dropped her jaw in astonishment.

"And that's it? You just like him?"

I didn't answer.

"What about him? How does he feel about you? Have you asked him? That's the most important part." Without taking her eyes off me, she twisted the cap off her bottle of tea and took a sip. "Did you tell him you like him?"

I still didn't answer.

"Come on. Why aren't you talking? This is your love life we're talking about. You get that, right? Are you listening to me?"

"I just don't want to talk about it right now," I told her, looking down.

Hijiri cocked her head to one side like she was puzzled, stared at me, then crossed her legs self-consciously.

"Yeah, because of your migraine? But wait, that's better now, right?" Hijiri said, in a flat voice. "Never mind—so did you tell him how you feel? That you like him?"

Once Hijiri realized that I wasn't going to answer, she laughed cautiously. "You being you, I'm guessing you haven't. Because you like it that way."

"Like it what way?" I asked.

"Come on, you know. You like doing things the easy way."

"Easy?" I said, sending the word back. "Easy how?"

"You know, the easy way. Not getting caught up in other people's lives, keeping everything to yourself, if you could have it your way."

"My way?" I asked.

"You always play it safe," Hijiri said. "I'm not saying that's a bad thing, okay? It's just the way you are, that's all. You're not the type of person who's willing to act—or maybe you can't. You tell me. Either way, it's obviously a lot of trouble for you to open up to somebody, to do something, to get involved, right? I mean, what if they misunderstood you? You'd be devastated, right? It would hurt, for sure. But if you just avoid the whole mess, bottle it up, at least you won't get hurt. Isn't that the way you like it?" Hijiri asked. "I'd call that easy. Just going through life without asking anything of anyone, or letting anyone ask anything of you. Sounds pretty easy to me."

"Is it, though?" I asked.

"How should I know?" Hijiri said. "That's for you to figure out. I'm not that kind of person. I've paid my dues." She recrossed her legs, slipped a pillow under herself, and lay down on her side, propping herself up on one elbow. "As I'm sure you're well aware, when a person cuts themself off from the world to live a quiet life, somebody somewhere has to pick up the slack. Someone has to take the hit."

". . . So you think people who do things the easy way, or what you're calling the easy way, aren't paying their dues like you?" I asked.

"I dunno," Hijiri said. "But from my perspective, it looks like a real good time, just coasting through life."

I looked at my fingers in silence.

"So what you're saying is . . . we all have to pay our dues, but, what, you've paid mine for me?" I asked her quietly.

Hijiri waited for a second. "Just forget about that. It isn't worth it. Let's talk about this precious love of yours. Does he feel the same way or not?" Her voice was oddly cheerful.

"I don't know," I confessed.

"Well, ask him," Hijiri said, exasperated. "See? How can you just sit there and do nothing?"

I told him how I feel, I said, before I had a chance to stop myself, but then I felt a dark cloud closing over me. Hijiri shot up and looked at me, eyes aglitter.

"Damn. You told him! What'd he say?"

"Nothing."

"He didn't say he liked you back?"

"It's not like that."

"Well, did you sleep together?"

I looked Hijiri in the face.

"It's not like that."

"If you haven't slept with him yet, you should give it a try," Hijiri said, kind of smirking. "It'll clear things up, at least. All kinds of things. You should do it. It'll get things moving. It's totally normal for the woman to take the lead with stuff like that."

I stared at her. She raised an eyebrow, looked at me, and laughed.

"You'll definitely get something out of your system. Maybe

you'll cry, or maybe you'll come. How can a teaspoon or two of bodily fluid make such a big difference? It makes no sense, I know. But it's super important. It's insane how important it is. So insane that sometimes I can't keep from laughing."

Hijiri gave me a pleading look. I was silent, but I didn't look away. It's not like that, I said again.

". . . There it is again. 'It's not like that.' What's that supposed to mean?" Hijiri asked. "You mean 'I'm not that kind of woman'?"

"I . . . I just like him, that's all," I said, in a voice too quiet for anyone to hear. "You must think I sound so stupid . . ."

I stopped, unsure what else to say, and pressed the bottle of tea to my lips to have a drink. I let out a sigh and looked down, then said a little more. I'm not sure what to say, I said. Maybe this is hard for you to understand, Hijiri. But it's not really about what I want to happen, or what I want to do—but that was all that I could get out.

"So maybe he doesn't feel the same way. Still, don't you want to sleep with him?" After Hijiri spoke, she sniffed once, loud enough for me to hear. "I mean, if you're totally opposed to ever sleeping with him, then forget I said anything. But you told him how you felt, right? To his face. So you definitely want something to happen on some level. I know that means something. Look, you owned your feelings, got shot down in a blaze of glory, and came home with your face a total mess. That's huge. You really put yourself out there. But now you're hiding in your safe place again, scared of getting hurt, and leaving everything up to him, wallowing in your own feelings like you're back in grade school, and for what? So that you can romanticize your desire and feel better about yourself? How's that working out for you? What are you scared of? What people think? You want men to think that you have something precious you're protecting? Or is it not the men you're worried about? Is that how you want to see yourself? I have to say, I think you're being grotesque."

". . . I hope you realize that not everyone in the world sees things the way you do."

I was shocked to hear these words come out of my mouth so naturally. Hijiri looked a little surprised too, judging by the way she looked at me. I sighed.

"Emotions are more complicated than that . . . The same goes for relationships," I said, struggling to get the words out. "Everyone has different priorities . . . Do you really think I need you to tell me if I'm doing it right?" I had to squeeze out every syllable. It almost felt like I was trying to convince myself.

"That's not what I'm saying." Hijiri frowned at me. "All I'm saying is, under the surface, you're full of the same base desires as the rest of us, and it pisses me off to see you all wrapped up in this little story that you've put together just because the truth is too much for you to handle. When I asked if you wanted to sleep with him, you looked at me like I was an idiot. What was that about? I don't know why you think you're so much better than I am, when I'm pretty sure you're wearing the underwear I gave you. That's all I'm saying. I can see what you're doing and it's disgusting."

"Whatever," I said. Then I said that I was done and shook my head. Hijiri said nothing, let out a sigh, then added this, almost as if she were speaking to herself.

"I swear, it pisses me off sometimes . . . Being around you."

A second later, I closed my eyes and summoned every ounce of power I had in me, thinking about Mitsutsuka. Thinking of his face, the way that Mitsutsuka's face looked when he smiled, I attempted to get back to the space we shared whenever we were together. *Fuyuko*. The sound of him saying my name, his worn-out polo shirt and the frayed corners of his shoulder bag, the color of the walls in the cafe, those drooping eyebrows, all the things he'd taught me about light, gathering together everything that I could find inside my head, inside my body, as I held my breath and tried to hold the feelings close to me, caging them in my arms, but it was so much that I thought I was going to burst into tears. It made me wish that I'd skipped the fancy restaurant, where I felt so out of place, forgotten about the wine, and met him at the cafe where we always met. We could have had sandwiches or spaghetti. Our cafe. The same place as always, the same seats at the same cafe, but we would celebrate, then talk about nothing, the way we always did, sitting across the table from one another. And if we wanted to drink, we could buy something at the convenience store and drink it in the park. I had no clue why I was thinking about these things. I sat there looking down, practically stuck to my chair, utterly consumed, but thinking these thoughts made it impossible to hold back the tears. I wanted to remember what Mitsutsuka had been like that night, when we were spending time together, only a few hours earlier, but something was standing in the way, blocking the memory. Something had come over Mitsutsuka's face, shifting under the streetlights and the darkness of the leaves, preventing it from coming into view. I tried to retrieve what I'd lost, what I'd felt with my fingers, the way he smelled, or the way we looked at each other, but somehow he was slipping further and further into the distance.

I rested my hands on the crown of my head and cried, but my hands had no heat to give. Did Mitsutsuka even remember me? I couldn't turn the terrible question off. I squeezed my eyes shut, sweeping my memory in the desperate pursuit of any trace connected in some way to Mitsutsuka. The Mitsutsuka who came back over from the stairs up to the platform, the Mitsutsuka whose smile was almost bashful, the Mitsutsuka who would happily talk to me about light for as long as I liked, whenever I asked. Mitsutsuka. It was getting hard to breathe. These thoughts raced through my mind, one after another, all the happy moments, the way that Mitsutsuka listened to every little thing I said and nodded patiently, the sight of him from behind, the way he walked, the way he thought, the way he talked, the clothes he wore, the smell of winter, all of it, because I really liked him, even though I knew nothing about him, and he knew nothing about me, and maybe that was all that this would ever come to, ending without getting off the ground, despite how good I knew it could be, had already been, with more good times than I knew what to do with, but as the days without him added up, I knew that I would burn through every last one of the memories, the anguish and the premonitions, the regrets, the gratitude, all of which would pass, never to return. I hugged my knees and cried. Hey, Hijiri said in a soft voice, there's nothing to cry about. She came over and worriedly rubbed my arm. I shook my head in silence. No, I said, or tried to say, but the word refused to come out. Hijiri looked like she was at a loss and told me she was really sorry. I couldn't get in touch with you, she said, I was worried, wondering if you were okay. I was upset, she said, but it's not like I came here to hurt your feelings, okay? I'm sorry, I'm so sorry, she said, sinking down onto the floor, still rubbing my arm. I didn't want to hurt your feelings, she said, crying with me. No, I said, you didn't say anything wrong, I'm the one who should apologize, I said, rubbing her arm back. No, Hijiri said, I was being nasty, I do it all the time. It messes everything up. I said some awful things to you, things I never should have said and didn't mean to say, she said, crying so hard that her makeup smeared. I understand, okay? I understand, I nodded, crying too. You probably think I don't know anything about you, Hijiri said, and honestly, that's fine, but I need you to know that I think of you as my friend, she said, almost too quietly for me to hear, her scrunched-up face covered in mucus and tears. I nodded. I want to know you better, she said. I want to know you, she cried, so I can be your friend, too. I slipped off the chair onto the floor and squeezed Hijiri's fingers, nodding through the tears.

13

H appy birthday!"

Sparkly balloons—one pink, two red—floated playfully just shy of the ceiling. The low table in the living room was soon filled with the assortment of side dishes that Hijiri had purchased at the department store marketplace, along with cake and chicken wrapped in aluminum foil, so we gave in and put the rest on the floor, then poured wine into glasses for a toast.

"Thirty-seven!" Hijiri said. "Can you believe it?"

Yeah, it's crazy, I said, then drank some of my wine. "Wait, should you really be drinking?" After taking a sip, I realized what we were doing and gave her a look.

"It's fine, trust me. It's not like I'll get drunk. Everybody's so uptight. I mean, I barely had a taste."

She set her glass of wine on the floor, then got a can of non-alcoholic beer from the fridge and poured it into a new glass, filling it to the brim. She drank the whole thing in one go, gulping loudly.

"God, this is the best," Hijiri said. "I don't even want to imagine what the last few months would have been like without this stuff. It's seriously the only thing getting me through this stupid pregnancy."

"Hey, nobody's stopping you. Go wild."

Hijiri had just entered her seventh month and was really starting to show. Forking up multiple slices of the salmon salad and putting them all in her mouth, she told me bitterly that, once her morning sickness had ended, her appetite shot through the roof. "My body's a total wreck. It's just one problem after another . . . Oh yeah, hold on," she said as she reached for her things and pulled out a plastic bag. Inside was a miniature Christmas tree, made of felt. She made a little space for it between the plates. "How's that for Christmas spirit?" she said, looking at me for approval.

"It's cute."

"Check out what happens when you press this," she said, touching a finger to a spot under the Christmas tree. Tiny lights started blinking. "Uh, it's kind of hard to tell if it's working right, but you get the idea," Hijiri laughed.

By the time we'd caught up on what was going on in our lives, we had eaten almost all of the food.

"Time really flies," Hijiri said, biting into the last piece of chicken with her front teeth. "It practically blows your hair off."

"I know what you mean. Everything happens so fast."

"I mean, my baby's going to be here in no time—by April, if all goes well. Spooky, right?"

A few months earlier, when Hijiri told me she was pregnant, I had questions. Wasn't she going to get married? Nope, she said. The guy evidently wasn't interested in having kids, so she thanked him for clarifying and broke up with him on the spot, resolved to have the child on her own.

"Things are pretty awful right now, but I'm excited to have my baby. Everyone keeps saying how hard it's going to be, but it's only making me more excited. They keep reminding me that this only seems like a good thing, that I don't know what I'm getting myself into. I mean, yeah, obviously. I haven't given birth yet," she laughed. "I like to do things my way, on my own—not like I need to tell you that. I don't know, I'm just thrilled, all the way down."

"How'd everything go with your mom?" I asked.

"Well, I dunno," Hijiri laughed, shaking her head. "We're pretty much not talking now. In her world, an unmarried woman having a kid on her own is worse than murder. She's just like, after all I did to raise you, how the hell did you turn out like this? Imagine saying that to your own daughter—who's practically forty, by the way."

"That's crazy," I shrugged.

"It's embarrassing. But maybe it's a good thing. She needs to get some distance from me. And I think I need to get away from her, too." Hijiri gave her belly a pat.

"I know, sweetie," she said with a smile. "It sounds like a lot, but this world isn't so bad, okay? Now hurry up and get born."

We walked to the station, side by side. At the gate, I waved until Hijiri had completely disappeared. I put my hands in the pockets of my jacket and walked down the road to my apartment, looking up into the night. One star was glowing faintly in the distance, and the whiteness of the winter moon gleamed from a cloudless sky. I walked through the deserted residential streets, coming to a main road, where I watched car after car pass by. The night had so many different lights. Over here, over there, my eyes chased after them, but it still made my chest ache.

Two years earlier, on the night of my birthday, Mitsutsuka never showed up.

I'd waited until dawn, outside of the cafe where we planned to meet, but Mitsutsuka never came. On my way back to the station, under a wintry morning sky so dark and blue it looked like it would never brighten, I felt a peculiar stillness in my heart.

After that, I pushed through the days without thinking about things, brought my workload back to normal, and occasionally met up with Hijiri to talk about work, or things that had nothing to do with work, slowly working my way back to the person I was before I started seeing Mitsutsuka. That makes it sound like there was a discernible before and after, but all I did was stop going to that cafe. Still, it took much longer than I'd expected to forget him.

And yet even that awful memory, which felt like it would crush my heart if only I would let it, the memory of that night, changed color day by day, so that when it snuck up on me, it took less and less time for my heart to settle down, until I finally felt the vortex in my heart growing smaller. It was bizarre to witness such vividly painful emotions, profound enough it felt like I could touch them, transform so completely.

I heard from Mitsutsuka only once, through a letter.

It was near the end of spring. Mitsutsuka confessed that he had lied. Fuyuko, the letter said, I lied to you about something incredibly important. I'm not actually a high school teacher. In handwriting I remembered all too well, he told me all about his life as he'd actually lived it, since losing his job at a food factory a few years earlier. Throughout the letter, he apologized multiple times. He said it pained him terribly. He also said that he thought it was best if we never met again.

I read that letter hundreds of times, and even visited the cafe on a handful of occasions. But I never saw him. Truly puzzled, I wrote him a letter myself, without even mentioning the content of the one he'd sent me, just a cheerful message, nice and light. I asked how things were going, told him about books that I was proofreading, that sort of thing. But once I'd folded it up, I realized that I didn't even have his address.

So spring went by, leading into summer, one day after another turning into night, then entering the morning, and before I knew it we were through the deep of autumn, back once again in winter. Soon, I started stepping out for long walks all the time, and not just around midnight on my birthday, but on other nights as well, and in the middle of the day, and in the morning. Walking through the light, in all its openness, like on that first night years before. When I was in the strong light of the morning or the day, I thought about it being midnight somewhere in the world, and thought about the people living there. People who spent their nights alone, alone through the night. When my thoughts went to Mitsutsuka, I held my breath, thinking about the time we'd spent talking together and how much I had liked him. Sometimes I started crying as I remembered everything, then slowly forgot again.

Back home, I washed the cups we'd used, balled up the foil and the plastic bags and tossed them in the trash, then wiped the table with a tightly wrung-out cloth. After that, I sat there in a blank state for some time, until something possessed me and I grabbed the CD player from the drawer. I put the earphones in my ears and pressed play. The memories crashed over me, and I held my breath as the same old feelings spread before my eyes. Squeezing my eyes shut against the onslaught of memories, I felt a pain pass through my chest over and over, and told myself that this would be the last time that I listened to the song. But the pain was already so far away. It was a pain that existed in memory, growing weaker by the day, a pain I was forgetting and would soon lose entirely. I closed my eyes and imagined myself grasping at the individual sounds with my fingertips, as if marking time and memory itself. Once I'd followed the dreamlike flashing trail to its conclusion and the last sound had gone away, I slowly opened my eyes.

I was trying to make progress with a galley, but a sleepy feeling hit me out of nowhere, and I changed into my pajamas and went to bed. I closed my eyes and let myself drift off into the darkness, but as I felt myself falling asleep, something shot through the haze. I rolled over and pulled the covers up, but I could feel something staring at me. I turned on the lamp by my bed and sat there with my eyes open, doing nothing for a moment. What was bothering me? What was going on? I stared up at the ceiling, completely still. For a while, I just sat there in that position, but eventually I gave up and was about to turn the lights off when it hit me. I knew what was stuck in my head. A phrase. Reaching for my desk, I grabbed the new notebook and pencil that were sitting by the edge and flipped the cover, lying flat on my back. Steadying the spine of the notebook with my palm, I took the pencil to the first blank page and wrote the words: "All the lovers in the night." The phrase had appeared out of nowhere. Through the faint light of the room, I looked over the words, which came together in the strangest way. On the one hand, they felt new to me, like something I'd never heard or seen before, though I also felt like maybe I had read them somewhere, in the title of a movie or a song, which meant it had emerged from someplace inside of me. Hard to say. Seeing my handwriting under the light, I realized that this was the first time I'd written something without having a specific purpose, not a comment in somebody else's manuscript or galley, but my own words on a blank sheet of paper. I had no clue what to do with these words, no idea what they were for, or what they meant, but I stared at them and felt them reach my heart and linger there. When I was done, I closed the notebook and switched off the light to find a shallow darkness spreading behind my eyelids. Now that the light was gone, I closed my eyes softly, knowing it would only be a short time until the light came back in the morning.

END